Endless Possibilities

using
NO-FAIL™
Methods

Nancy Johnson-Srebro

Published by:
Silver Star, Inc.
55 Saddle Lake Rd.
Tunkhannock, PA 18657

Exclusive Distributor

C&T Publishing, Inc. • P.O. Box 1456 • Lafayette, CA 94549
(800) 284-1114 • Website:www.ctpub com

ISBN 0-9645469-0-6
Printed in China
10 9 8 7 6 5

Dedication

To My Mother, Ruby Garrison Johnson

I've often thought how wonderful it is when a mother and daughter or daughter-in-law share the love of quilting. And I am happy to say that my mother at the young age of 64 has finally asked me to teach her quilt-making! One of her recent comments was, "I don't have time to cook, sleep or go to the grocery store. I just want to stay home and quilt".

Acknowledgements

As I've traveled down the road of life there are many people who have touched me and are special each in their own way. I would like to thank the following people:

My children, Mark, Alan, Karen and my husband, Frank. I couldn't do this without you.

Karen Brown, Maria Carr, Debbie Grow, Pat Holly, Cheryl Kagen, Laurie Mace, Janet McCarroll, Marcia Rickansrud, Roxanne Sidorek, Sandy Storz and Ethel Whalen - for their friendship and continued support of my writing.

Lea Wang, who so passionately put in innumerable hours to quilt the wallhangings in this book.

Jim Brogan, who started it all by showing me my computer's "on" switch.

Steve Appel, one terrific photographer. All of the blocks and quilts were photographed by Steve.

Conrad Associates, Clarks Summit, Pennsylvania. Their computer and graphic skills never cease to amaze me.

Russ Tarleton - A friend and advocate.

Special Thanks to the following companies for providing various quilting supplies:

Clotilde
(Fine Silk Pins)
B 3000
Louisiana, MO 63353

Warm Products, Inc.
(Batting)
954 E. Union Street
Seattle, WA 98122

Nextdoor Neighbor Dyeworks
(Hand Dyed Fabrics)
5201 Blackjack Mountain Road
Mansfield, AR 72944

Fasco/Fabric Sales Co., Inc.
(Fabrics)
6250 Stanley Ave. So.
Seattle, WA 98108

Mountain Mist®
(Batting)
100 Williams St.
Cincinnati, OH 45215

Cherrywood Fabrics, Inc.
(Hand Dyed Fabrics)
P.O. Box 486
Brainerd, MN 56401

The Stencil Company
(Quilting Stencils)
28 Castlewood Dr.
Cheektowaga, NY 14227

Hobbs Bonded Fibers
(Batting)
200 Commerce St.
Waco, TX 76702

Alaska Dyeworks
(Hand Dyed Fabrics)
300 W. Swanson Ave.
Wasilla, AK 99654

Omnigrid® Inc.
(Rulers and Mats)
1560 Port Drive
Burlington, WA 98233

Quilter's Rule Intl, LLC.
817 Mohr Ave.
Waterford, WI 53185

Bernina® of America
(1530 Sewing Machine)
3500 Thayer Court
Aurora, IL 60504

Table of Contents

Patterns

Cutting and sewing directions for a 6" finished and a 12" finished block are given for each pattern. The 6" rotary cutting measurements are featured in parentheses in each pattern.

* = beginner pattern
** = intermediate pattern

My Fellow Quilters,

There are many books that share the basics of rotary cutting and modern piecing techniques. Both recent innovations have revolutionized the quilting art. I have written several of these books, and other good works have been authored by a few of my friends who teach quiltmaking at the national level. Bookshelves in Fabric and Quilt Shops are loaded and literally sagging with books on these elementary techniques.

So why have I written this book? It's not my purpose to write yet another work on rotary cutting and piecing, for the many such books already on the market delve thoroughly into these topics. My objective, then, in this book is different and is a bit unique. In *Endless Possibilities* I share those secrets that will bring your present skills to a higher level. And they will help you turn what would otherwise become an average, "everyday" miniature, wallhanging or quilt project into a real "masterpiece"! Also, I've developed several NO-FAIL™ methods after making thousands of miniatures and over one hundred quilts. As a quilt teacher and author, I feel it is my job to encourage you and share as much as I know. I don't hold secrets back. Whether I'm writing, teaching or lecturing, I have always felt that I am working for you, not the other way around. So if you've ever spent precious time ripping out seams and trying to fudge pieces together, you need this book! It builds on most all of the basic quilting instruction books on the market today.

Here are some of my NO-FAIL™ methods that will allow you to create the very highest quality work: You *CAN* get an accurate 1/4" seam allowance for you and your machine, and you *CAN* get an accurate 1/4" stop when mitering corners on borders and bindings, and when working with 30°, 45° and 60° diamonds. I also share the most incredible NO-FAIL™ method for setting in triangles and squares when you are working with stars. Lastly, I have included my NO-FAIL™ Fabric Yardage Chart. With this Yardage Chart, you will never have to guess how much fabric to buy for your next quilting project. No more panic trips when you run short, hoping that there's still some fabric at the shop. Also, you'll never again have the expense of buying extra fabric just to make sure you have enough. (Note: A tablet of my NO-FAIL™ Fabric Yardage Charts is available at your local quilt shop. Plan to take it along on your next fabric buying trip.)

You will also find twenty patterns in two popular sizes, **6"** and **12"**, for a total of **forty** blocks. While drafting these patterns, I realized how different they looked before, and after, I colored them with my fabric color choices. After some thought, I realized how valuable an "uncolored" graphic of each block would be. So I have included this special feature throughout the pattern section. Please feel free to trace over the uncolored quilt blocks; mix and match them until your heart is content. You can literally make thousands of one-of-a-kind quilts and wallhangings from these patterns. Or if you are inclined to make a full size quilt using only one of the blocks, you can simply refer to my Fabric Guide for Making Full Size Quilts in the back of the book. My books are written to make your quilting life easier, not harder!

Nancy

Back Tacking - After sewing forward, stop and put the sewing machine in reverse and stitch backwards three stitches.

Butting Seams - This is a technique to press the seam allowances opposite each other. (See Diagram 1.) The seam allowance on the top unit is pressed to the left and the seam allowance on the bottom unit is pressed to the right.

Diagram 1

Dog Ears - This term refers to the fabric excess that is formed at opposite corners when you sew two geometric shapes together. You will create dog ears when you sew two half square triangles, quarter square triangles, 45° and 60° diamonds, trapezoids, etc. together. An exception is when you sew squares or rectangles together - no dog ears are created because the sides are exactly at 90° to each other.

Press - To use an iron to smooth out the wrinkles in your fabric. When quilters talk about pressing they frequently joke that you iron blue jeans but you press quilt blocks. The NO-FAIL™ methods that follow will help you achieve perfect pressing every time:

STEP ONE: Place stitched units on the ironing board so that the seam allowance is facing you (toward your body). Gently press the seams together to set the stitches. This will flatten any slight distortions that result from the machine's thread tension.

STEP TWO: After pressing to set the stitches, gently open the piece and press from the right side of the fabric. Set the iron on the pieced unit, do not move the iron around. Any movement will tend to stretch or push the pieced unit out of its true shape.

If you are pressing long seams such as lattice strips or borders, you must complete one additional step to prevent stretching and/or creating a curve in the strips:

STEP THREE: First follow Steps One and Two. After setting the iron on the pieced strip, you will move the iron in a slight zig-zag direction along the length of the seam, rather than using a side-to-side direction. (See Diagrams 2A, 2B and 2C.) Keep your thumb beneath the strip and your four finger tips should make a finger press ahead of the iron. This NO-FAIL™ method will give you perfect straight strips every time.

Diagram 2C

Diagram 2B

Diagram 2A

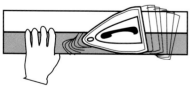
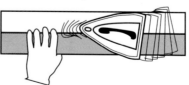
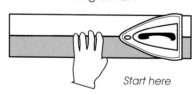

Start here

Your equipment is critical to the quality of your finished quilt. Here are the equipment choices I have found to be the best for me.

Rulers - Omnigrid rulers are the most accurately printed rulers I've found. If you are not sure that your ruler is printed correctly, stand it against or behind an Omnigrid ruler and see if all the markings line up. If the markings align, you're in great shape; if they don't, you should not use this ruler for precision quiltmaking.

Cutting Mats - Consider buying a mat that reverses from a dark color to a light color. You will then be able to use the side that creates the greatest contrast between your fabric and the mat. This helps reduce eye fatigue. I prefer to use the OMNIMAT.

Multi View Lense - This lens is made by Quilter's Rule International and I can't get along without it. You need to make only one of the blocks in this book and view it through the Multi View Lense to see it multiplied twenty-five times! You can see your full-size quilt before making it!

Straight Pins - I've found that the #5004 IBC Fine Silk Pins by Clotilde work the best. A few years ago I did extensive pin research because of the following problem: I was creating a big hump after pinning my butted pieces together, and my sewing machine would not smoothly sew over this section. After some thought, I realized that conventional straight pins were too large in diameter.

It's important to understand how critical the placement of your straight pin is in relation to where the seam is butted. You should always place the pin a hair (about 1/16" or a bit less) ahead of the butted seams. (See Diagram 3A.)

If you place the pin exactly in the butted seams, you will separate the seams by a small amount equal to the diameter of the pin. (See Diagram 3B.) This is a common problem when butting and pinning the center of an Eight Pointed Star block. Oftentimes its center doesn't quite match. You may have seen this problem in your own projects.

Diagram 3A

The pin is offset from the butted seam by 1/16".

Diagram 3B

Do not pin directly into the butted seam allowance.

Sewing Machine - Use a machine that is in good running condition and you are comfortable with. Consider using a presser foot that is open, allowing you to see the sewing area. This is critical for accurate work, especially when setting in triangles and squares in Star patterns.

Sewing Machine Needle - I like to use a size 11 (Metric 75) needle in my machine. It pierces the fabric cleanly instead of pushing the fibers apart. Another thing - change those needles frequently!

Thread - I use a good quality 100% cotton thread while machine piecing. After countless hours of work, I don't want my quilt to fall apart because I've saved a few cents on poor quality thread.

For An Accurate 1/4"
Seam Allowance

Getting an exact 1/4" seam allowance has challenged quiltmakers since day one! If your blocks are measuring between 1/8" and 1/4" undersize or oversize, the problem is probably in your seam allowance. After following this simple NO-FAIL™ method for getting an accurate 1/4" seam allowance, you will never have a problem with blocks that are off-size.

STEP ONE: (See Diagram 4) Position the point of the needle so it is ready to enter the hole in the throat plate. Place a long piece of 1/4" masking tape on the throat plate so that the needle just *barely touches* the left edge of the masking tape.

STEP TWO: (See Diagram 5) Now butt another piece of 1/4" tape to the right of the first piece of tape. Run the tape *just up to* the front edge of the feed dog.

STEP THREE: (See Diagram 6) Remove the first piece of tape. The distance from the edge of the tape to the needle should be 1/4".

| Diagram 4 | Diagram 5 | Diagram 6 |

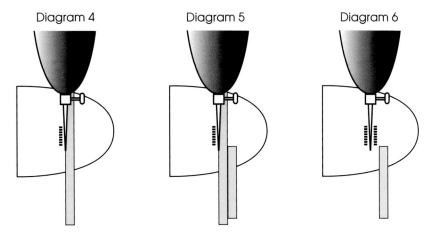

Sewing Test: You <u>must</u> do a sewing test to be sure you have an accurate 1/4" seam allowance for you and your machine. Here is the test I always ask the students to try before beginning their class project:

Cut one 2 7/8" square. Cut in half diagonally, once. While gently butting against the tape, sew the two triangles together to make a square. Press. Place the ruler on top of the square. It <u>must</u> measure 2 1/2" x 2 1/2". (You lose 3/8" in a diagonal seam allowance: 2 7/8" - 3/8" = 2 1/2")

If your test square is not coming out exactly on size, move the tape until you get an accurate 2 1/2" square. Most people are surprised to learn they need a <u>scant</u> 1/4" seam allowance.

STEP FOUR: After you have found the proper 1/4" seam allowance for you and your machine, place several layers (6-8) of 3/4" wide masking tape or packing tape directly over the 1/4" tape. You want to create a ridge to butt against, so the fabric will not ride over the top of the tape.

Note: If you own a sewing machine with a front loading bobbin case, or a machine with a removable tray, this method can still work for you. Once you have built up your layers of tape, simply take a craft knife or put an old blade in your rotary cutter and cut the tape where necessary. When you close your machine or put the tray back on, the two separate pieces of tape will still match.

One of the secrets I always share in class is how to get an exact ¼" stop when working with star diamonds. I also use this NO-FAIL™ Method when I want mitered borders and bindings on my quilts.

There are three steps to a perfect ¼" stop when using my NO-FAIL™ Method:

STEP ONE: Position two 45° diamonds right sides together. With the wrong side facing you, gently butt the diamonds against the tape. Start sewing exactly at the top of the diamonds (See Diagram 7). Continue sewing until you come to what you think is ¼" from the bottom of the diamonds. Stop sewing with the needle a <u>quarter</u> of the way into the diamonds. Don't go so far that you engage the bobbin. You don't want to create a stitch (See Diagram 8).

STEP TWO: Lift the presser foot up and turn the diamonds to see if they butt against the tape (See Diagram 9). If the diamonds butt against the tape, you have a perfect ¼" stop.

| Diagram 7 | Diagram 8 | Diagram 9 |

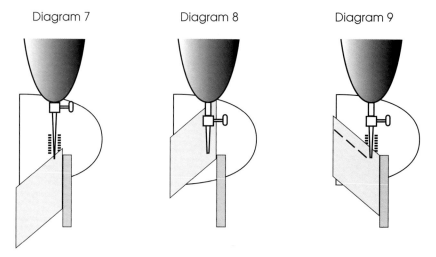

If your diamonds don't butt up against the tape or they extend over the tape, you do not have a perfect ¼" stop. To fix this problem, lift the presser foot up and turn the handwheel clockwise until the needle comes out of the fabric (remember you didn't create a stitch when you stopped sewing in Step One). Carefully move the diamonds until they butt against the tape. Once this is done, lower the presser foot and turn the handwheel counter-clockwise so that <u>three quarters </u>of the needle is in the fabric. Continue on to Step Three.

STEP THREE: Turn the fabric back to the position shown in Diagram 8 and put the machine in reverse and back tack three stitches. You now have a perfect ¼" stop. The seam allowance will match when you are setting in your squares and triangles because you are using the same tape seam allowance guide.

These NO-FAIL™ methods will save you countless hours of ripping out when you are setting in triangles and squares on your next star pattern. I will use an Eight Pointed Star <u>with</u> perfect 1/4" stops (See page 8) to show you the four steps.

SETTING IN TRIANGLES -
Number the wrong sides of the star diamonds and triangles. (See Diagram 10)

Diagram 10

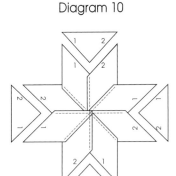

STEP ONE: Align and pin side #1 of the diamond with the #1 side of the triangle (See Diagram 11). The triangle is hidden beneath the diamond.

As you pin in towards the diamond seam, you will notice the triangle is 1/4" too long. Don't panic, this is correct. *With the wrong side (#1) of the diamond facing you,* butt the pieces against the tape you are using as a guide for your 1/4" seam allowance, and start sewing from the upper tip towards the diamond seam. As you sew in towards the diamond seam, gently move it out of the way. **Stop sewing 1/16" from the diamond seam and back tack.** (If you sew into the diamond seam allowance, you will form a little pleat on the front side of the diamond).

Diagram 11

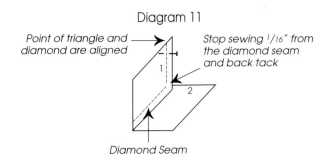

Point of triangle and diamond are aligned

Stop sewing 1/16" from the diamond seam and back tack

Diamond Seam

STEP TWO: With the *wrong side (#2) of the triangle facing you,* align and pin the triangle point to the diamond point (See Diagram 12). Butt the pieces against the tape and start sewing from the outside towards the diamond seam.

As you sew in towards the diamond seam, gently move it out of the way. **Stop sewing 1/16" from the diamond seam and back tack.** Press toward the triangle and cut off the dog ears.

Diagram 12

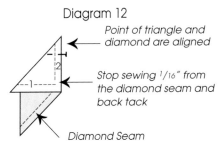

Point of triangle and diamond are aligned

Stop sewing 1/16" from the diamond seam and back tack

Diamond Seam

SETTING IN SQUARES - Number the wrong sides of the diamonds and squares. (See Diagram 13).

Diagram 13

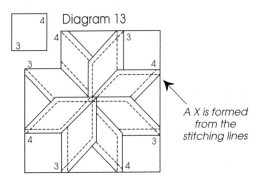

A X is formed from the stitching lines

STEP THREE: With the right sides together, align and pin the #3 side of the square to the #3 side of the diamond. (As you do this, you will notice the square will also align with the outside edge of the *triangle* and the *#3 side* of the diamond). As you pin in towards the diamond seam also notice the #3 side of the square is 1/4" too long. Again, don't panic, this is correct.

With the *wrong side of the diamond* facing you, butt the pieces against the tape and start sewing from the outside towards the diamond seam. As you sew in towards the diamond seam, gently move it out of the way. **Stop sewing 1/16" from the diamond seam and back tack.**

STEP FOUR: (See Diagram 13) With the right sides together, align and pin the #4 side of the square to the #4 side of the diamond. With the *wrong side of the square facing you,* start sewing from the outside towards the diamond seam. As you sew in towards the diamond seam, gently move it out of the way. **Stop sewing 1/16" from the diamond seam and back tack.** Press toward the square.

HINT: By pressing towards the triangles and squares, a X is formed from the stitching lines at the points of the diamond. When sewing the blocks to lattice strips, you will be able to see where to just miss sewing into the diamond points. (See Diagram 13).

For Using The NO-FAIL™
Fabric Yardage Chart
Copyright Silver Star, Inc.

Part A

COLUMN 1 - Refer to your pattern for this information. You should include the reference letter of the shape and the color that is specified.

COLUMN 2 - Your pattern will supply this information (measure the templates including the seam allowance). Remember that (two) half square triangles, or (four) quarter square triangles equal (one) square. You _must_ convert any fractions into decimal measurements. If you're not sure how to do this, refer to my Fraction/Decimal Conversion Chart on Page 11.

COLUMN 3 - Multiply the number of shapes required in Column 2 by the total number of quilt blocks needed.

COLUMN 4 - Divide the width of the fabric (I always use 40" for 100% cotton fabric) by the length (L) of the shape in Column 2. Be sure to _ROUND DOWN_ to the nearest whole number.

Note: If using 45° diamonds, 60° diamonds, equilateral triangles or parallelograms, you must calculate (draw on paper) how many of the desired shapes will fit on a 40" strip.

COLUMN 5 - Divide Column 3 by Column 4. Be sure to _ROUND UP_ to the nearest whole number.

COLUMN 6 - Refer to Column 2 for the height (H) of the shape.

COLUMN 7 - To determine the total inches of fabric required, multiply the whole number in Column 5 by the height indicated in Column 6. _ROUND UP_ to the nearest whole number.

Example

12" Monkey Wrench Block

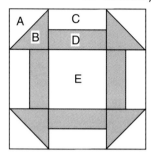

A - Cut 2 - 3 $7/8$ Squares
    Cut in half diagonally.
B - Cut 2 - 3 $7/8$ squares
    Cut in half diagonally.
C - Cut 4 - 2" x 6 $1/2$" rectangles
D - Cut 4 - 2" x 6 $1/2$" rectangles
E - Cut 1 - 6 $1/2$" square

Sample NO-FAIL™ Yardage Chart For A 30 Block Monkey Wrench Quilt

Column 1	Column 2	Column 3	Column 4	Column 5	Column 6	Column 7
Letter and Color (Refer to Pattern)	How Many of This Shape Per Block and Shape Dimensions (H x L)	Total Number of This Shape Needed for 30 Blocks In The Quilt	Shapes Available Per Strip (40" ÷ Length) Round Down to Nearest Whole Number	Total Strips Needed (Col. 3 ÷ Col. 4) Round Up to Nearest Whole Number	Height of The Shape (Refer to Col. 2)	Total Inches (Col. 5 x Col. 6) Round Up to Nearest Whole Number
A - Light	2 Squares 3.875" x 3.875"	60	10 per Strip (40 ÷ 3.875)	6 Strips Needed (60 ÷ 10)	3.875 (3 7/8")	24"
B - Dark	2 Squares 3.875" x 3.875"	60	10 per Strip (40 ÷ 3.875)	6 Strips Needed (60 ÷ 10)	3.875 (3 7/8")	24"
C - Light	4 Rectangles 2" x 6.5"	120	6 per Strip (40 ÷ 6.5)	20 Strips Needed (120 ÷ 6)	2	40"
D - Dark	4 Rectangles 2" x 6.5"	120	6 per Strip (40 ÷ 6.5)	20 Strips Needed (120 ÷ 6)	2	40"
E - Light	1 Square 6.5" x 6.5"	30	6 per Strip (40 ÷ 6.5)	5 Strips Needed (30 ÷ 6)	6.5 (6 1/2")	33"

Part B

Column 1A - List the color, letter and number of inches required for each shape.

Column 1B - Total the inches of each color.

Column 1C - Convert the total inches of each color into yards. Refer to my Helpful Figures Chart on page 11.

HINT: To be sure you don't run short of fabric due to shrinkage and resquaring, always add a bit extra to the total yards needed.

Sample Chart for Converting Total Inches Into Total Yards for A 30 Block Monkey Wrench Quilt

Column 1A	Column 1B	Column 1C
List the Color, Letter and Number of Inches Required of Each Shape See Column 7	Total Inches of Each Color	Total Yards Needed (Refer to the Helpful Figures Chart)
Light - A, C, E, - 24" + 40" + 33"	97"	2 3/4 yds.
Dark - B, D - 24" + 40"	64"	1 7/8 yds.

NO-FAIL™

Fabric Yardage Chart
Copyright Silver Star, Inc.

Part A

Column 1	Column 2	Column 3	Column 4	Column 5	Column 6	Column 7
Letter and Color (Refer to Pattern)	How Many of This Shape Per Block and Shape Dimensions (H x L)	Total Number of This Shape Needed for ___ Blocks In The Quilt	Shapes Available Per Strip (40" ÷ Length) Round Down to Nearest Whole Number	Total Strips Needed (Col. 3 ÷ Col. 4) Round Up to Nearest Whole Number	Height of The Shape (Refer to Col. 2)	Total Inches (Col. 5 x Col. 6) Round Up to Nearest Whole Number

Part B

Column 1A	Column 1B	Column 1C
List the Color, Letter and Number of Inches Required of Each Shape (See Column 7)	Total Inches of Each Color	Total Yards Needed (Refer to the Helpful Figures Chart)

Fraction/Decimal Conversion Chart

$1/8$ = .125
$1/4$ = .25
$3/8$ = .375
$1/2$ = .5
$5/8$ = .625
$3/4$ = .75
$7/8$ = .875

Helpful Figures Chart

These measurements (inches) are rounded up to the next whole number.

$1/8$ yd. = 5"	$1 1/8$ yds. = 41"	$2 1/8$ yds. = 77"	$3 1/8$ yds. = 113"	$4 1/8$ yds. = 149"
$1/4$ yd. = 9"	$1 1/4$ yds. = 45"	$2 1/4$ yds. = 81"	$3 1/4$ yds. = 117"	$4 1/4$ yds. = 153"
$3/8$ yd. = 14"	$1 3/8$ yds. = 50"	$2 3/8$ yds. = 86"	$3 3/8$ yds. = 122"	$4 3/8$ yds. = 158"
$1/2$ yd. = 18"	$1 1/2$ yds. = 54"	$2 1/2$ yds. = 90"	$3 1/2$ yds. = 126"	$4 1/2$ yds. = 162"
$5/8$ yd. = 23"	$1 5/8$ yds. = 59"	$2 5/8$ yds. = 95"	$3 5/8$ yds. = 131"	$4 5/8$ yds. = 167"
$3/4$ yd. = 27"	$1 3/4$ yds. = 63"	$2 3/4$ yds. = 99"	$3 3/4$ yds. = 135"	$4 3/4$ yds. = 171"
$7/8$ yd. = 32"	$1 7/8$ yds. = 68"	$2 7/8$ yds. = 104"	$3 7/8$ yds. = 140"	$4 7/8$ yds. = 176"
1 yd. = 36"	2 yds. = 72"	3 yds. = 108"	4 yds. = 144"	5 yds. = 180"

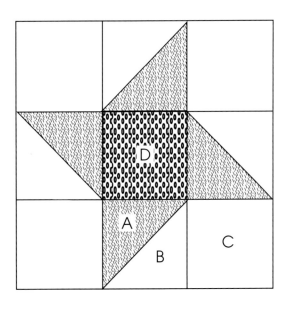

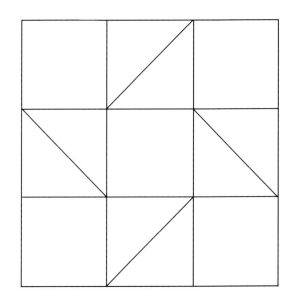

Block Size:
12" (or 6") finished

Seam Allowance:
¼"

Full Size
Quilt Guide:
Page 59

Photo on Page 36

Identifying the Shapes

A, B - Half Square Triangle
C, D - Square

Rotary Cutting Directions

Numbers in parentheses are for the 6" block.

A - Cut 2 - 4 ⁷/₈" squares, medium dark. (2 ⁷/₈")
Cut in half diagonally, once.

B - Cut 2 - 4 ⁷/₈" squares, light. (2 ⁷/₈")
Cut in half diagonally, once.

C - Cut 4 - 4 ¹/₂" squares, light. (2 ¹/₂")

D - Cut 1 - 4 ¹/₂" square, dark. (2 ¹/₂")

Sewing Directions

Arrows show pressing direction.

1. Sew **A** to **B**. Cut off the dog ears.
Press. Make four sets.

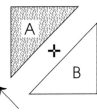

2. Pin and sew into rows. Press according to the diagram. Butt, pin and sew the rows together. Press according to the side arrows.

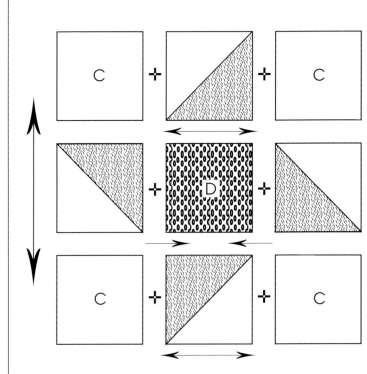

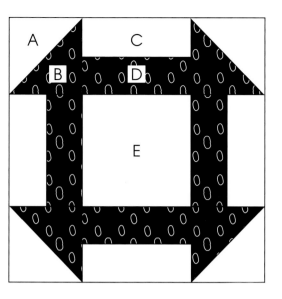

Block Size:
12" (or 6") finished

Seam Allowance:
¼"

Full Size Quilt Guide:
Page 59

Photo on Page 35

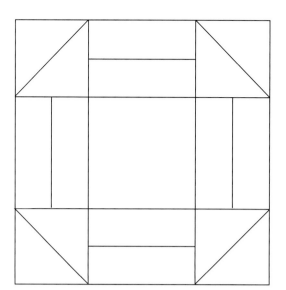

Identifying the Shapes

A, B - Half Square Triangle
C, D - Rectangle
E - Square

Rotary Cutting Directions

Numbers in parentheses are for the 6" block.

A - Cut 2 - 3 ⁷/₈" squares, light. (2 ⁷/₈")
   Cut in half diagonally, once.

B - Cut 2 - 3 ⁷/₈" squares, dark. (2 ⁷/₈")
   Cut in half diagonally, once.

C - Cut 1 - 2" x 28" strip, light. (1 ¹/₂" x 12")

D - Cut 1 - 2" x 28" strip, dark. (1 ¹/₂" x 12")

E - Cut 1 - 6 ¹/₂" square, light. (2 ¹/₂") Another
   option for the 12" block is to use one of the
   other 6 ¹/₂" unfinished blocks from this book.

Sewing Directions

Arrows show pressing direction.

1. Sew **A** to **B**. Cut off the dog
   ears. Press. Make four sets.

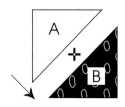

2. Sew strip **C** to strip **D**. Press. Cut into four 6 ¹/₂"
   rectangles. (2 ¹/₂")

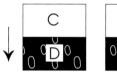

3. Pin and sew into rows. Press according to the
   diagram. Butt, pin and sew the rows together.
   Press according to the side arrows.

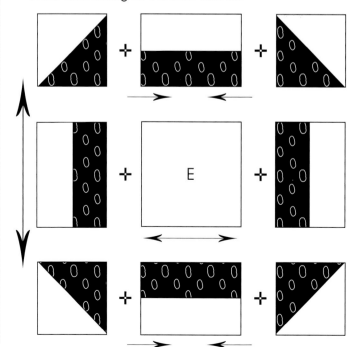

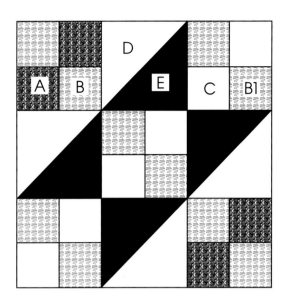

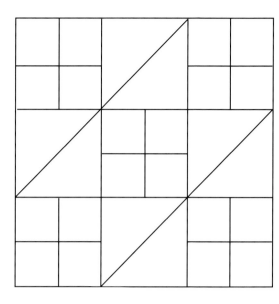

Block Size:
12" (or 6") finished

Seam Allowance:
¼"

Full Size
Quilt Guide:
Page 59

Photo on Page 35

Identifying the Shapes

A, B, B1, C - Square
D, E - Half Square Triangle

Rotary Cutting Directions

Numbers in parentheses are for the 6" block.

A - Cut 1 - 2 ¹/₂" x 12" strip, medium dark.
(1 ¹/₂" X 7")

B - Cut 1 - 2 ¹/₂" x 12" strip, medium light.
(1 ¹/₂" X 7")

B1 - Cut 1 - 2 ¹/₂" x 17" strip, medium light.
(1 ¹/₂" x 10")

C - Cut 1 - 2 ¹/₂" x 17" strip, light. (1 1/2" x 10")

D - Cut 2 - 4 ⁷/₈" squares, light. (2 ⁷/₈")
Cut in half diagonally, once.

E - Cut 2 - 4 ⁷/₈" squares, dark. (2 ⁷/₈")
Cut in half diagonally, once.

Sewing Directions

Arrows show pressing direction.

1. Sew strip **A** to strip **B**. Press. Cut the sewn strips into four 2 ¹/₂" sections. (1 ¹/₂")

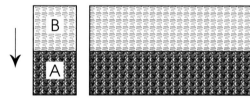

2. Butt, pin and sew the **A/B** sections together. Press. Make two sets.

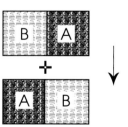

3. Sew strip **B1** to strip **C**. Press.
   Cut the sewn strips into six 2 1/2" sections. (1 1/2")

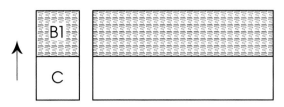

4. Butt, pin and sew the **B1/C** sections together.
   Press. Make three sets.

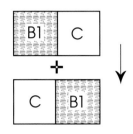

5. Sew **D** to **E**. Cut off the dog ears. Press.
   Make four sets.

6. Pin and sew into rows. Press according to the diagram. Butt, pin and sew the rows together. Press according to the side arrows.

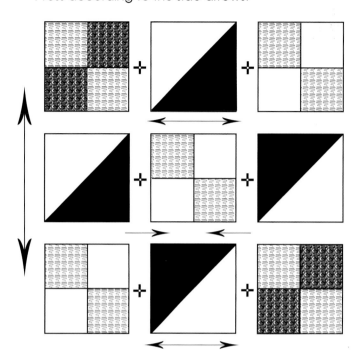

A totally different look is created when you turn every other Jacob's Ladder block.

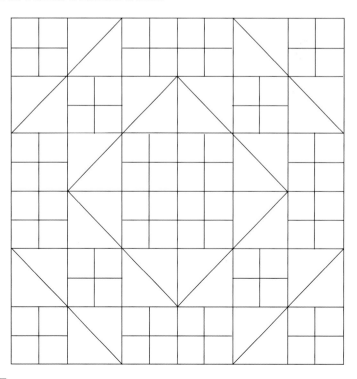

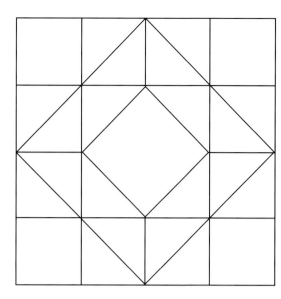

Block Size:
12" (or 6") finished

Seam Allowance:
¼"

Full Size
Quilt Guide:
Page 60

Photo on Page 34

Identifying the Shapes

A, B, C, D - Half Square Triangle
E, F - Square

Rotary Cutting Directions

Numbers in parentheses are for the 6" block.

A - Cut 4 - 3 ⁷/₈" squares, medium light. (2 ³/₈")
Cut in half diagonally, once.

B - Cut 2 - 3 ⁷/₈" squares, medium dark. (2 ³/₈")
Cut in half diagonally, once.

C - Cut 2 - 3 ⁷/₈" squares, contrasting medium
dark. (2 ³/₈") Cut in half diagonally, once.

D - Cut 2 - 3 ⁷/₈" squares, light. (2 ³/₈")
Cut in half diagonally, once.

E - Cut 1 - 4 ³/₄" square, dark. (2 ⁵/₈")

F - Cut 4 - 3 ¹/₂" squares, dark. (2")

Sewing Directions

Arrows show pressing direction.

1. Sew **A** to **B**. Cut off the dog ears. Press.
Make four sets.

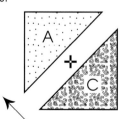

2. Sew **A** to **C**. Cut off the dog ears. Press.
Make four sets.

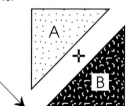

3. Butt, pin and sew one **A/B** set to the **A/C** set. Press. Make four sets.

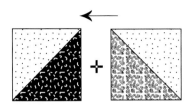

4. Following the diagram, sew **D** to the opposite sides of **E**. Press to **D**. Add **D** to the other two sides of **E**. Press. Cut off the dog ears.

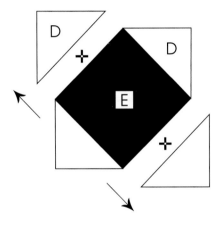

5. Pin and sew into rows. Press according to the diagram. Butt, pin and sew the rows together. Press according to the side arrows.

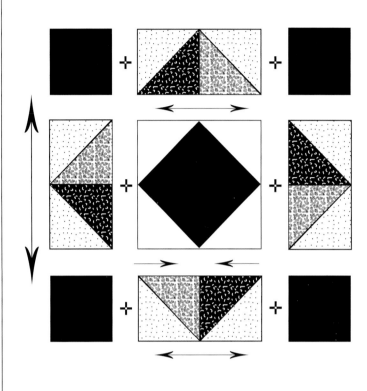

You can see endless possibilities with the Squares and Triangles pattern depending on where you position your fabric.

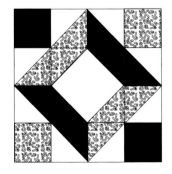  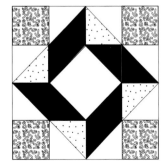 

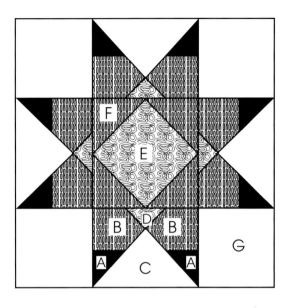

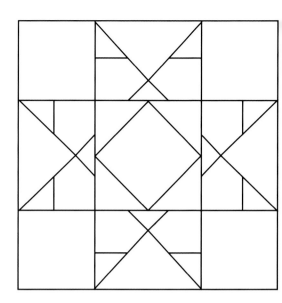

Block Size:
12" (or 6") finished

Seam Allowance:
¼"

Full Size
Quilt Guide:
Page 60

Photo on Page 34

Identifying the Shapes

A, F - Half Square Triangle
B - Single Prism
C, D - Quarter Square Triangle
E, G - Square

Rotary Cutting Directions

Numbers in parentheses are for the 6" block.

A - Cut 4 - 2 ³/8" squares, dark. (1 ⁵/8")
Cut in half diagonally, once.

B - Cut 1 - 2 ¹/2" x 26" strip, medium dark.
(1 ¹/2" x 18") Cut into eight 2 ¹/2" x 3 ¹/8"
rectangles. (1 ¹/2" x 1 ⁷/8") To recut each
rectangle into a single prism, use a 6" square
Omnigrid® ruler. Measure in 1 ¹/4" (³/4") from
the 2 ¹/2" (1 ¹/2") side of the rectangle. Put a
pencil mark on the top and bottom of the
rectangle. Place the 6" ruler diagonally on the
rectangle. You will notice the 45° line runs
through the pencil marks. Cut off the excess
fabric.

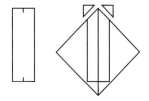

C - Cut 1 - 6 ¹/4" square, light. (3 ³/4") Cut in half
diagonally, twice.

D - Cut 1 - 3 ¹/4" square, medium light. (2 ¹/4")
Cut in half diagonally, twice.

E - Cut 1 - 4 ¹/16" square, medium light. (2 ⁵/16")
(4 ¹/16" is located between 4" and 4 ¹/8")
(2 ⁵/16" is located between 2 ¹/4" and 2 ³/8")

F - Cut 2 - 3 ³/8" squares, medium dark. (2 ¹/8")
Cut in half diagonally, once.

G - Cut 4 - 4" squares, light. (2 ¹/4")

Sewing Directions

Arrows show pressing direction.

1. Following the diagram, sew **A** to **B**. Press.
Cut off the dog ears. Make four sets of each.

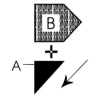 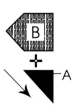

2. Sew the correct **A/B** set to the **C** triangle. Press. Cut off the dog ears. Make four sets.

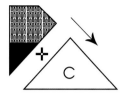

3. Sew **D** to the remaining **A/B** set. Press. Cut off the dog ears. Make four sets.

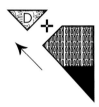

4. Butt, pin and sew the two sections together. Press to the **A/B/C** section. Cut off the dog ears. Make four sets.

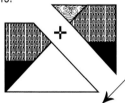

5. Following the diagram, sew an **F** to the opposite sides of **E**. Press to **F**. Add **F** to the other two sides of **E**. Press. Cut off the dog ears.

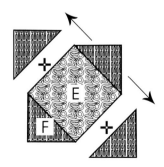

6. Pin and sew into rows. Press according to the diagram. Butt, pin and sew the rows together. Press according to the side arrows.

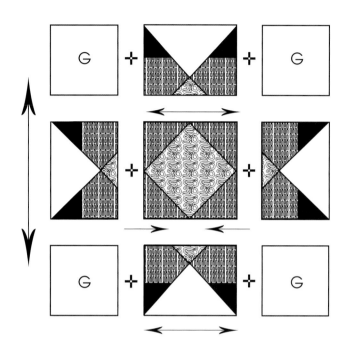

The Amherst Star pattern is named after the Amherst Museum Quilters Guild from Amherst, New York.

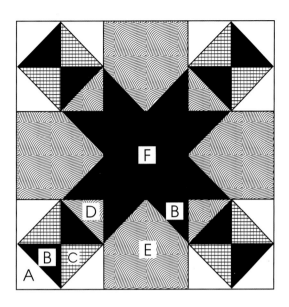

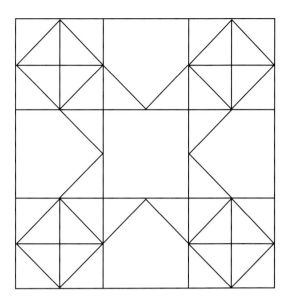

Block Size:
12" (or 6") finished

Seam Allowance:
¼"

Full Size
Quilt Guide:
Page 60

Photo on Page 35

Identifying the Shapes

A, B, C, D - Half Square Triangle
E - Single Prism
F - Square

Rotary Cutting Directions

Numbers in parentheses are for the 6" block.

A - Cut 6 - 2 ⁷/₈" squares, light. (1 ⁷/₈")
Cut in half diagonally, once.

B - Cut 8 - 2 ⁷/₈" squares, dark. (1 ⁷/₈")
Cut in half diagonally, once.

C - Cut 4 - 2 ⁷/₈" squares, medium dark. (1 ⁷/₈")
Cut in half diagonally, once.

D - Cut 2 - 2 ⁷/₈" squares, medium light. (1 ⁷/₈")
Cut in half diagonally, once.

E - Cut 4 - 4 ¹/₂" x 4 ⁵/₈" rectangles, medium light.
(2 ¹/₂" x 2 ⁵/₈") To recut each rectangle into a
single prism, use a 6" square Omnigrid® ruler.
Measure in 2 ¹/₄" (1 ¹/₄") from the 4 ¹/₂" (2 ¹/₂")
side of the rectangle. Put a pencil mark on the
top and bottom of the
rectangle. Place the
6" ruler diagonally on

the rectangle. You will notice the 45° line runs
through the pencil marks. Cut off the excess
fabric.

F - Cut 1 - 4 ¹/₂" square, dark. (2 ¹/₂")

Sewing Directions

Arrows show pressing direction.

1. Sew **A** to **B**. Cut off the dog ears. Press.
Make four sets.

2. Sew **A** to **C**. Cut off the dog ears. Press.
Make eight sets.

3. Sew **B** to **D**. Cut off the dog ears. Press. Make four sets.

4. Following the diagram, butt, pin and sew the **A/B, A/C, B/D** sets together. Press according to the arrows. Then press the center seam according to the side arrows. Make two sets of each.

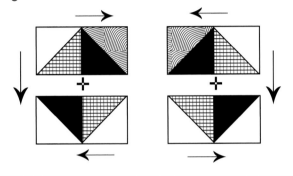

5. Sew one **B** to **E**. Press. Sew **B** to the other side of **E**. Press. Cut off the dog ears. Make four sets.

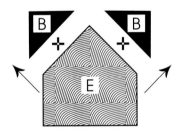

6. Pin and sew into rows. Press according to the diagram. Butt, pin and sew the rows together. Press according to the side arrows.

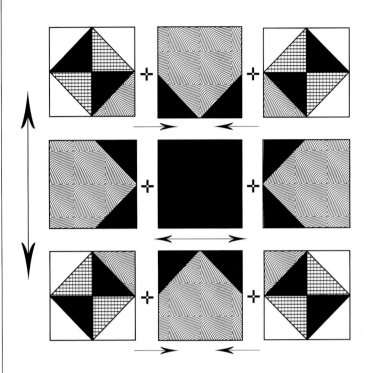

A secondary design is formed when you sew four Bursting Star blocks together.

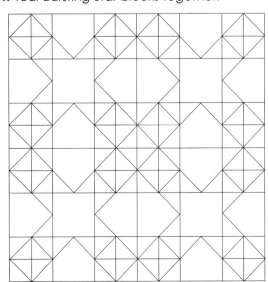

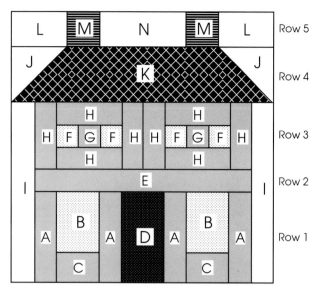

Row 5
Row 4
Row 3
Row 2
Row 1

Block Size:
12" (or 6") finished

Seam Allowance:
¼"

Full Size
Quilt Guide:
Page 61

Photo on Page 36

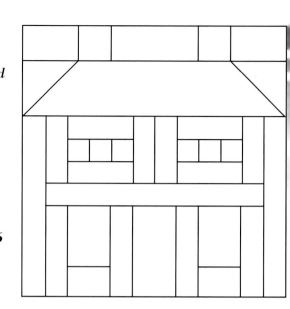

Identifying the Shapes

A, B, C, D, E, H, I, L, N - Rectangle
F, G, M - Square
J - Half Square Triangle
K - Full Trapezoid

Rotary Cutting Directions

Numbers in parentheses are for the 6" block.

A - Cut 4 - 1 1/2" x 4 1/2" rectangles, medium dark.
(1" x 2 1/2")

B - Cut 2 - 2 1/2" x 3 1/4" rectangles, medium light.
(1 1/2" x 1 3/4")

C - Cut 2 - 1 3/4" x 2 1/2" rectangles, medium dark.
(1 1/4" x 1 1/2")

D - Cut 1 - 2 1/2" x 4 1/2" rectangle, dark.
(1 1/2" x 2 1/2")

E - Cut 1 - 1 1/2" x 10 1/2" rectangle, medium dark.
(1" x 5 1/2")

F - Cut 4 - 1 1/2" squares, medium light. (1")

G - Cut 2 - 1 1/2" squares, medium dark. (1")

H - Cut 8 - 1 1/2" x 3 1/2" rectangles, medium dark.
(1" x 2")

I - Cut 2 - 1 1/2" x 8 1/2" rectangles, light.
(1" x 4 1/2")

J - Cut 1 - 3 3/8" square, light. (2 1/8")
Cut in half diagonally, once.

K - Cut 1 - 3" x 13 1/4" rectangle, contrasting dark. (1 3/4" x 7 1/4") To recut into a full trapezoid, use a 6" square Omnigrid® ruler. Place the ruler so the 45° line is in the corner of the rectangle. Also keep the 45° line on the bottom of the rectangle. Cut off the excess fabric. Slide the ruler to the other corner of the rectangle and cut off the excess fabric.

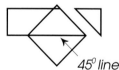 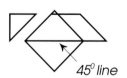

45° line   *45° line*

L - Cut 2 - 2" x 3" rectangles, light. (1 1/4" x 1 3/4")

M - Cut 2 - 2" squares, contrasting medium dark.
(1 1/4")

N - Cut 1 - 2" x 4 1/2" rectangle, light. (1 1/4" x 2 1/2")

Sewing Directions

Arrows show pressing direction.

ROW 1:

1. Sew **B** to **C**. Press. Make two sets.

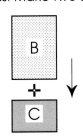

2. Sew one **A** to each side of the **B/C** set. Press. Make two sets.

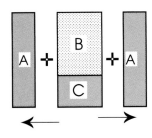

3. Sew one of the **A/B/C** sets to each side of **D**. Press.

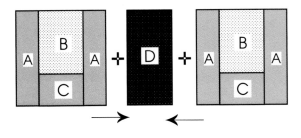

4. Sew **Row 1** to **E (Row 2)**. Press to **Row 2, (E)**.

ROW 3:

5. Sew one **F** to each side of **G**. Press. Make two sets.

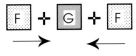

6. Sew one **H** to the top and bottom of the **F/G** set. Press. Make two sets.

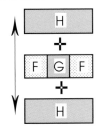

7. Sew and press according to the diagram.

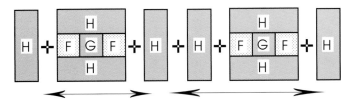

8. Sew **Row 3** to **(Row 2) E**. Press to **Row 2 (E)**.

9. Sew **I** to each side of the sewn **Row 1, 2** and **3** unit. Press to **I**.

ROW 4:

10. Sew one **J** to each side of **K**. Press. Cut off the dog ears.

11. Sew **Row 4** to **Row 3**. Press to **Row 4**.

ROW 5:

12. Sew and press according to the diagram.

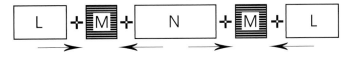

13. Sew **Row 5** to **Row 4**. Press to **Row 5**.

The Campbell House pattern is named after my friend, Bonnie Campbell, from Fairfax, VA.

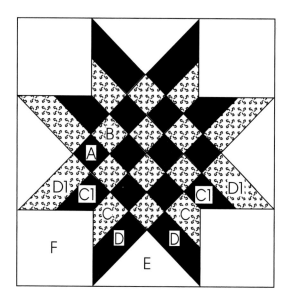

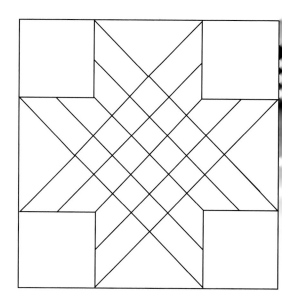

Block Size:
12" (or 6") finished

Seam Allowance:
¼"

Full Size
Quilt Guide:
Page 61

Photo on Page 35

Identifying the Shapes

A, B, F - Square
C, C1, D, D1 - Left and Right Half Trapezoids
E - Quarter Square Triangle

Rotary Cutting Directions

Numbers in parentheses are for the 6" block.

A - Cut 2 - 1 3/4" x 9" strips, dark. (1 1/8" x 6")

B - Cut 2 - 1 3/4" x 9" strips, medium dark.
(1 1/8" x 6")

C - Cut 4 - 1 3/4" x 3 1/8" rectangles, medium dark.
(1 1/8" x 2") *Cut two rectangles into left half
trapezoids and two rectangles into right half
trapezoids.

C1 - Cut 4 - 1 3/4" x 3 1/8" rectangles, dark.
(1 1/8" x 2") *Cut two rectangles into left half
trapezoids and two rectangles into right half
trapezoids.

D - Cut 4 - 1 3/4" x 4 3/8" rectangles, dark.
(1 1/8" x 2 5/8") *Cut two rectangles into left half
trapezoids and two rectangles into right half
trapezoids.

D1 - Cut 4 - 1 3/4" x 4 3/8" rectangles, medium dark.
(1 1/8" x 2 5/8") *Cut two rectangles into left half
trapezoids and two rectangles into right half
trapezoids.

*Note: *Position one C on top of one C1 with wrong sides
together. To recut into left and right half trapezoids,
use a 6" square Omnigrid® ruler. Place the ruler so the
45° line is in the corner of the rectangle. Also keep the
45° line on the bottom of the rectangle. Cut off the
excess fabric. When you separate the two pieces, you
will have one left half trapezoid and one right
half trapezoid. Do the same with D and D1 rectangles.*

Left Handed Quilters   Right Handed Quilters

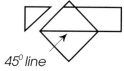

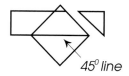

45° line   *45° line*

E - Cut 1 - 6 1/4" square, light. (3 3/4")
Cut in half diagonally, twice.

F - Cut 4 - 4" squares, light. (2 1/4")

Sewing Directions

Arrows show pressing direction.

1. **Checkered Section** - Sew and press strip **A** and **B** according to the diagram. Make sure you press after adding each strip. The strip will measure 5 1/2" in height. (3") Cut the sewn strips into four 1 3/4" sections. (1 1/8")

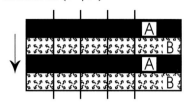

2. Butt, pin, sew and press the sections together according to the diagram.

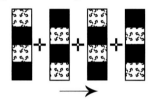

3. **Point Section** - Sew **D1** to **C1**. Sew **C** to **D**. Start sewing the **D1/C1** section to the **C/D** section. Stop sewing 1/4" from the bottom edge and back tack. Make two sets. You will press these seams when you are butting it to the middle section in #4.

Stop sewing 1/4" and back tack

4. Press the seams in the point section opposite of the checkered section. Cut off the dog ear. Butt, pin and sew one point section to each end of the checkered section. Press to the checkered section. This is now the middle section.

5. **Side Section** - Sew **D** to **C**. Sew **C1** to **D1**. Start sewing the **D/C** section to the **C1/D1** section. Stop sewing 1/4" from the bottom edge and back tack. Make two sets. You will press these seams when you are butting to the checkered section in #7.

Stop sewing 1/4" and back tack

6. Sew **E** to the sides of the points. Press. Cut off the dog ears. Make two sets.

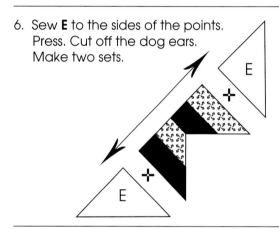

7. Press the seams of the points opposite of the checkered section. Cut off the dog ears. Butt, pin and sew the side sections to the middle section. Press to the side sections.

8. Set in the **F** squares according to the directions on page 9. Press to the **F** squares.

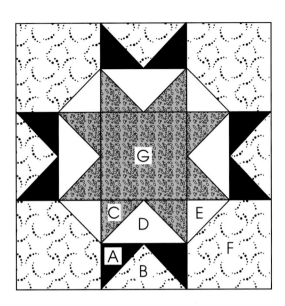

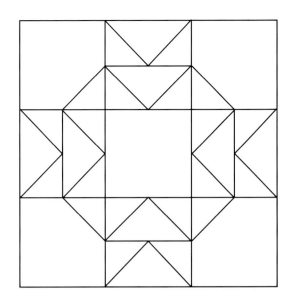

Block Size:
12" (or 6") finished

Seam Allowance:
¼"

Full Size
Quilt Guide:
Page 61

Photo on Page 34

Identifying the Shapes

A, C, E - Half Square Triangle
B, D - Quarter Square Triangle
F - Clipped Square
G - Square

Rotary Cutting Directions

Numbers in parentheses are for the 6" block.

A - Cut 4 - 2 ⁷/₈" squares, dark. (1 ⁷/₈")
   Cut in half diagonally, once.

B - Cut 1 - 5 ¹/₄" square, medium light. (3 ¹/₄")
   Cut in half diagonally, twice.

C - Cut 4 - 2 ⁷/₈" squares, medium dark. (1 ⁷/₈")
   Cut in half diagonally, once.

D - Cut 1 - 5 ¹/₄" square, light. (3 ¹/₄")
   Cut in half diagonally, twice.

E - Cut 2 - 2 ⁷/₈" squares, light. (1 ⁷/₈")
   Cut in half diagonally, once.

F - Cut 4 - 4 ¹/₂" squares, medium light. (2 ¹/₂")
   To cut a clipped square, place the ruler so the
   1 ¹¹/₁₆" marking runs diagonally through the
   square. (¹⁵/₁₆") (1 ¹¹/₁₆" is located between
   1 ⁵/₈" and 1 ³/₄".) (¹⁵/₁₆" is located between ⁷/₈"
   and 1".) Cut off the excess fabric.

Left Handed Quilters   Right Handed Quilters

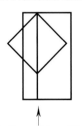   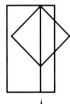

1 ¹¹/₁₆" marking (¹⁵/₁₆")   *1 ¹¹/₁₆" marking (¹⁵/₁₆")*

G - Cut 1 - 4 ¹/₂" square, medium dark. (2 ¹/₂")

Sewing Directions

Arrows show pressing direction.

1. Sew one **A** to **B**. Press. Sew **A** to the other side of **B**.
   Press. Cut off the dog ears. Make four sets.

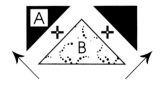

2. Sew one **C** to **D**. Press. Sew **C** to the other side of **D**. Press. Cut off the dog ears. Make four sets.

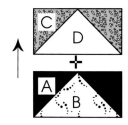

3. Sew the **C/D** set to the **A/B** set. Press. Make four units.

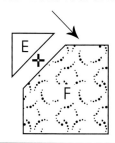

4. Sew **E** to **F**. Press. Make four sets.

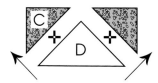

5. Butt, pin and sew into rows. Press. Butt, pin and sew the rows together. Press according to the side arrows.

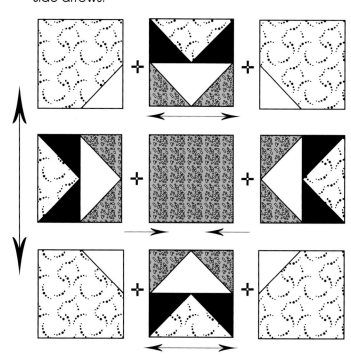

A great scrappy quilt can be made using different fabrics for the inside stars.

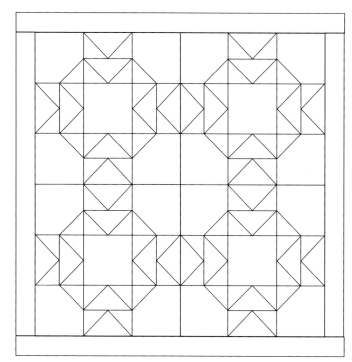

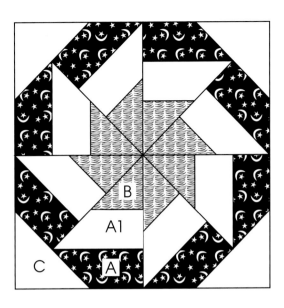

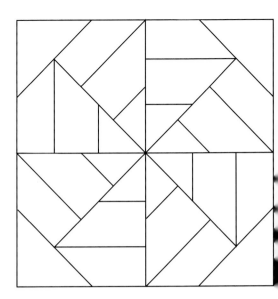

Block Size:
12" (or 6") finished

Seam Allowance:
¼"

**Full Size
Quilt Guide:**
Page 62

Photo on Page 34

Identifying the Shapes

A, A1 - Single Prism (See #2)
B, C - Half Square Triangle

Rotary Cutting Directions

Numbers in parentheses are for the 6" block.

A - Cut 1 - 2 ¼" x 44" strip, dark. (1 ³/₈" x 25")

A1 - Cut 1 - 2 ¼" x 44" strip, light. (1 ³/₈" x 25")

B - Cut 4 - 3 ³/₈" squares, medium dark. (2 ¹/₈")
Cut in half diagonally, once.

C - Cut 2 - 4 ³/₈" squares, light. (2 ⁵/₈")
Cut in half diagonally, once.

Sewing Directions

Arrows show pressing direction.

1. Sew strip **A** to strip **A1**. Press. The height of the sewn strips will measure 4". (2 ¹/₄") Cut the sewn strips into eight 4 ⁷/₈" sections. (2 ³/₄")

2. To recut each rectangle into a single prism, use a 6" square Omnigrid® ruler. Place the 6" ruler diagonally on the rectangle so the 45° line runs through the seam. Cut off the excess fabric. **(Keep the light fabric, A1, to the right while cutting.)**

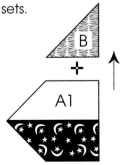

3. Sew **B** to **A1**. Press. Cut off the dog ears. Make eight sets.

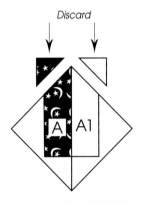

4. Following the diagram, sew and press two of the
   A/A1/B sets together. Cut off the dog ears.
   Make four sets.

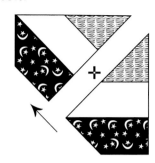

5. Butt, pin, sew and press two sets together to
   make a half. Make two sets.

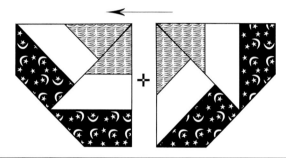

6. Butt, pin and sew the two halves together.
   It doesn't matter which way you press the center
   seam. Add **C** to the four corners. Press.
   Cut off the dog ears.

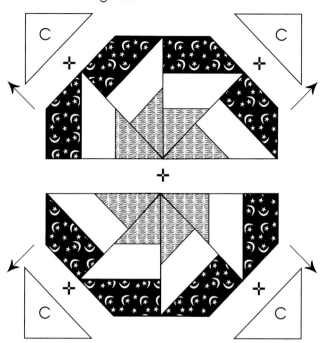

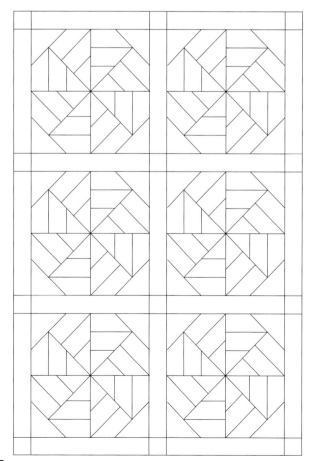

If you alternate the colors for the B shape, you will create a pinwheel for the center of the Ferris Wheel.

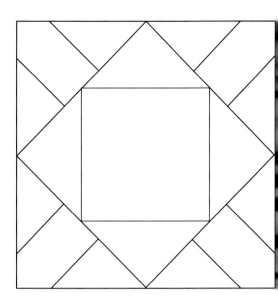

Block Size:
12" (or 6") finished

Seam Allowance:
1/4"

**Full Size
Quilt Guide:**
Page 62

Photo on Page 35

Identifying the Shapes

A - Square
B - Half Square Triangle
C - Quarter Square Triangle
D - Single Prism

Rotary Cutting Directions

Numbers in parentheses are for the 6" block.

A - Cut 1 - 6 1/2" square, light. (3 1/2")
Note: *Another option for the 12" block is to use one
of the 6 1/2" unfinished blocks from this book.*

B - Cut 2 - 5 1/8" squares, dark. (3")
Cut in half diagonally, once.

C - Cut 2 - 5 1/2" squares, medium dark. (3 3/8")
Cut in half diagonally, twice.

D - Cut 4 - 3" x 4 7/8" rectangles, medium light.
(1 3/4" x 2 3/4") To recut each rectangle into a
single prism, use a 6" square Omnigrid® ruler.
Measure in 1 1/2" (7/8") from the side of the
rectangle. Put a pencil mark on the top and
bottom of the rectangle. Place the 6" ruler

diagonally on the rectangle. You will notice the
45° line runs through the pencil marks. Cut off
the excess fabric.

45⁰ line

Sewing Directions

Arrows show pressing direction.

1. Following the diagram, sew **B** to the opposite sides
   of **A**. Press to **B**. Add **B** to the other two sides of **A**.
   Press. Cut off the dog ears.

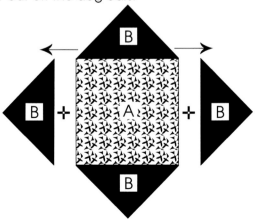

2. Sew **C** to the sides of **D**. Press. Make four sets.

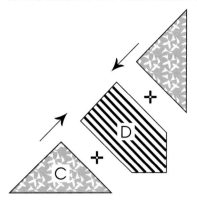

3. Sew one **C/D** set to the opposite sides of the **A/B** center. Press to the **C/D** set. Add the other **C/D** sets to the other two sides of the **A/B** center. Press. Cut off the dog ears.

*A wonderful scrap quilt can be made simply by changing the centers (A) of the blocks.
Also, the striped fabric creates a secondary design!*

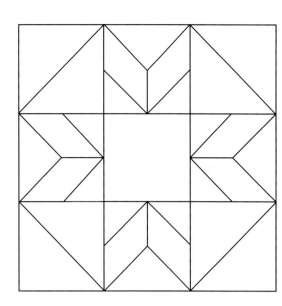

Block Size:
12" (or 6") finished

Seam Allowance:
¼"

**Full Size
Quilt Guide:**
Page 62

Photo on Page 36

Identifying the Shapes

A, A1 - Parallelogram
B, D, E - Half Square Triangle
C - Quarter Square Triangle
F - Square

Rotary Cutting Directions

Numbers in parentheses are for the 6" block.

A - Cut 1 - 2 ¹/₂" x 15" strip, dark. (1 ¹/₂" x 10")

A1 - Cut 1 - 2 ¹/₂" x 15" strip, dark. (1 ¹/₂" x 10")

Position the **A** strip on top of the **A1** strip, wrong sides together. With the right side facing you, make four 1 ⁷/₈" diagonal cuts. (1 ¹/₄") Separate the parallelograms. You will have four **A**s and four **A1**s. See the diagram.

Left Handed Quilters   Right Handed Quilters

B - Cut 4 - 2 ⁷/₈" squares, medium dark. (1 ⁷/₈") Cut in half diagonally, once.

C - Cut 1 - 5 ¹/₄" square, light. (3 ¹/₄") Cut in half diagonally, twice.

D - Cut 2 - 4 ⁷/₈" squares, dark. (2 ⁷/₈") Cut in half diagonally, once.

E - Cut 2 - 4 ⁷/₈" squares, light. (2 ⁷/₈") Cut in half diagonally, once.

F - Cut 1 - 4 ¹/₂" square, dark. (2 ¹/₂")

Sewing Directions

Arrows show pressing direction.

1. Sew **A** to **A1**. Stop sewing ¹/₄" from the bottom edge and back tack. Press. Cut off the dog ears. Make four sets.

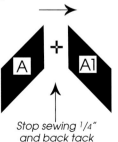

*Stop sewing ¹/₄"
and back tack*

2. Sew **B** to one side of the **A/A1** set. Press. Sew **B** to the other side. Press. Cut off the dog ears. Make four sets.

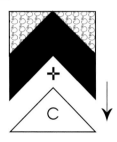

3. Set in the **C** triangles according to the directions on page 9. Press. Cut off the dog ears. Make four units.

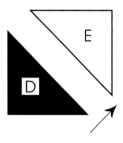

4. Sew **D** to **E**. Cut off the dog ears. Press. Make four sets.

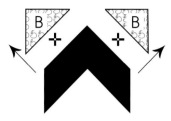

5. Butt, pin and sew into rows. Press according to the diagram. Butt, pin and sew the rows together. Press according to the side arrows.

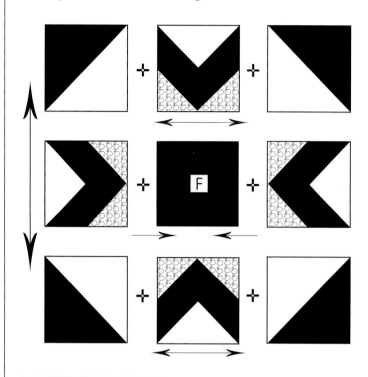

The pattern, Love Apple Star, is named after The Love Apple Quilters Guild from Cherry Hill, New Jersey. I have had the pleasure of working with this Guild many times.

Squares and Triangles
Pattern on page 16

Star of Dreams
Pattern on page 48

Pinwheel Star
Pattern on page 44

Double Pointed Star
Pattern on page 26

Ferris Wheel
Pattern on page 28

Amherst Star
Pattern on page 18

Star Lane
Pattern on page 50

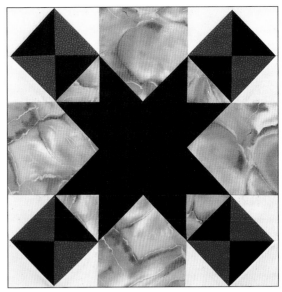

Bursting Star
Pattern on page 20

Checkered Star
Pattern on page 24

Jacob's Ladder
Pattern on page 14

Indian Head
(Shown with a 6" Star of Dreams center)
Pattern on page 30

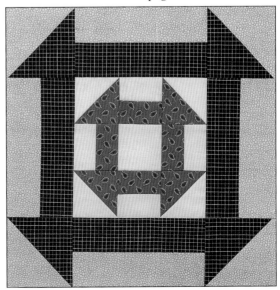

Monkey Wrench Times Two
(Shown with a 6" Monkey Wrench center)
Pattern on page 13

Star Surrounded
Pattern on page 52

Peek-A-Boo Star
Pattern on page 42

Love Apple Star
Pattern on page 32

Campbell House
Pattern on page 22

Friendship Star
Pattern on page 12

Tic Tac Toe
(Shown with a 6" Amherst Star center)
Pattern on page 56

Swamp Patch
Pattern on page 54

Square Within
Pattern on page 46

"Beach Houses" made and quilted by Debbie Grow. This charming wallhanging uses the Campbell House pattern. The fabrics and strip pieced fences add a whimsical touch.

"Revolving Ferris Wheels" made by Debbie Grow. Quilted by Lea Wang. The assortment of solid fabrics makes a striking statement. The Ferris Wheel block appears as if it is spinning!

"Floral Latticework" made by Debbie Grow. Quilted by Lea Wang. The use of striped fabric makes this wallhanging appear intricate, but there are simply nine 12" Indian Head blocks with 6" Friendship Star centers. A marvelous secondary design is formed by the striped fabric.

"Light Star Eruption" made and quilted by Ethel Whalen.

"Black Star Eruption" made by the author. Quilted by Lea Wang.

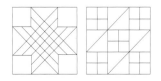

This original setting by Ethel Whalen uses three blocks: 6" Jacob's Ladder, 6" and 12" Checkered Stars. The position of the blocks gives an impression that the center star is erupting! It is fascinating how different colors can make the same design appear totally different.

"Stars Adrift" made by the author. Quilted by Lea Wang. The Star Surrounded and Square Within blocks were used to create this dazzling wallhanging.

"Blinking Stars" made by the author. Quilted by Lea Wang. The 6" Amherst Stars (minus the G squares) in the lattice strips, appear to float amongst the Double Pointed Stars.

"A Friendly Neighborhood" made by Marcia Rickansrud. Quilted by Lea Wang. Marcia used the 12" Campbell House and 6" Friendship Star to create a wonderful "folk artsy" sampler. She embellished the sampler by adding appliquéd trees, hearts and even a swing! The fence and flag are strip pieced.

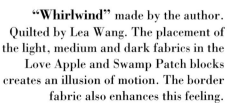

"Whirlwind" made by the author. Quilted by Lea Wang. The placement of the light, medium and dark fabrics in the Love Apple and Swamp Patch blocks creates an illusion of motion. The border fabric also enhances this feeling.

"Victorian Beauty" made by the author. Quilted by Lea Wang. This original setting is by Janet McCarroll.

The Peek-A-Boo Star is set alternately with a block consisting of four quarter square triangles, thus forming an Ohio Star!

"Monkey Wrench Times Two" made by the author. Quilted by Lea Wang. The array of striped and plaid fabrics turns this traditional pattern into a feast for the quilter's eyes. I also designed an exciting border, allowing me to expand the blocks into it.

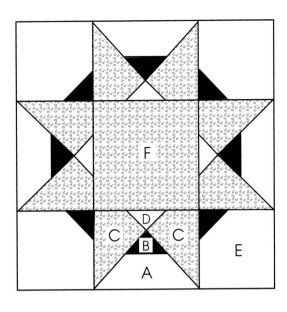

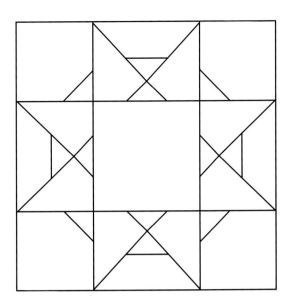

Block Size:
12" (or 6") finished

Seam Allowance:
¼"

Full Size
Quilt Guide:
Page 62

Photo on Page 36

Identifying the Shapes

A - Full Trapezoid
B - Half Square Triangle
C - Kite
D - Quarter Square Triangle
E - Clipped Square
F - Square

Rotary Cutting Directions

Numbers in parentheses are for the 6" block.

A - Cut 4 - 1 3/4" x 6 1/4" rectangles, light.
(1 1/8" x 3 3/4") To recut each rectangle into a
full trapezoid, use a 6" square Omnigrid® ruler.
Place the ruler so the 45° line is in the corner of
the rectangle. Also keep the 45° line on the
bottom of the rectangle. Cut off the excess
fabric. Slide the ruler to the other corner of the
rectangle and cut off the excess fabric.

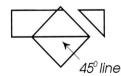 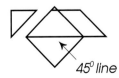

45° line   *45° line*

B - Cut 4 - 2 5/8" squares, dark. (1 3/4") Cut in half
diagonally, once.

C - Cut 4 - 4 3/8" squares, medium dark. (2 5/8")
Cut in half diagonally, once. To cut a kite shape,
use a 6" square Omnigrid® ruler. Place the 4 3/8"
mark (2 5/8") on the tip of the half square
triangle. Cut off the excess fabric.

Left Handed Quilters   Right Handed Quilters

4 3/8"   4 3/8"

D - Cut 1 - 3 1/4" square, light. (2 1/4")
Cut in half diagonally, twice.

E - Cut 4 - 4" squares, light. (2 1/4") To cut a clipped
square, place the ruler so 1 1/2" marking runs
diagonally through the square. (7/8") Cut off the
excess fabric.

Left Handed Quilters   Right Handed Quilters

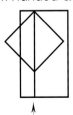   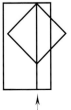

1 1/2" marking (7/8")   *1 1/2" marking (7/8")*

F - Cut 1 - 5 1/2" square, medium dark. (3")

Arrows show pressing direction.

1. Sew **B** to **A**. Press. Cut off the dog ears.
   Make four sets.

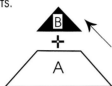

2. Sew **C** to the **A/B** set. Press. Cut off the dog ears.
   Make four sets.

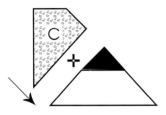

3. Sew **D** to **C**. Press. Cut off the dog ears.
   Make four sets.

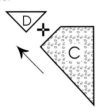

4. Sew the **A/B/C** set to the **C/D** set. Press.
   Cut off the dog ears. Make four units.

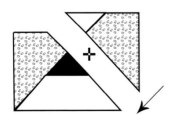

5. Sew **B** to **E**. Press. Cut off the dog ears.
   Make four sets.

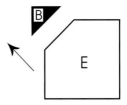

6. Pin and sew into rows. Press according to the
   diagram. Butt, pin and sew the rows together.
   Press according to the side arrows.

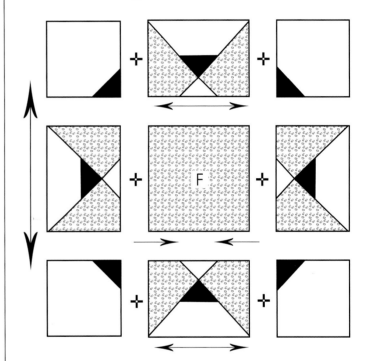

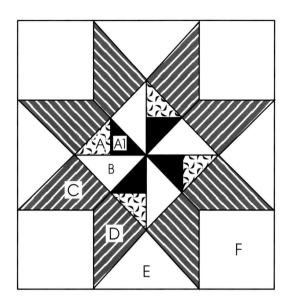

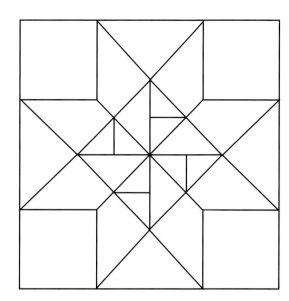

Block Size:
12" (or 6") finished

Seam Allowance:
¼"

**Full Size
Quilt Guide:
Page 63**

Photo on Page 34

Identifying the Shapes

A, A1 - Quarter Square Triangle
B - Half Square Triangle
C - Right Half Trapezoid
D - Left Half Trapezoid
E - Quarter Square Triangle
F - Square

Rotary Cutting Directions

Numbers in parentheses are for the 6" block.

A - Cut 1 - 3 ³/₄" square, contrasting, medium dark. (2 ¹/₂")
Cut in half diagonally, twice.

A1 - Cut 1 - 3 ³/₄" square, dark. (2 ¹/₂")
Cut in half diagonally, twice.

B - Cut 2 - 3 ³/₈" squares, light. (2 ¹/₈")
Cut in half diagonally, once.

C - Cut 4 - 3" x 4 ³/₈" rectangles, medium dark. (1 ³/₄" x 2 ⁵/₈") *Cut each into a right half trapezoid.

D - Cut 4 - 3" x 4 ³/₈" rectangles, medium dark. (1 ³/₄" x 2 ⁵/₈") *Cut each into a left half trapezoid.

*Note: *Position one **C** on top of one **D** with wrong sides together. To recut into left and right half trapezoids, use a 6" square Omnigrid® ruler. Place the ruler so the 45° line is in the corner of the rectangle. Also keep the 45° line on the bottom of the rectangle. Cut off the excess fabric. When you separate the two pieces, you will have one left half trapezoid and one right half trapezoid. Repeat with rest of **C** and **D** rectangles.*

Left Handed Quilters   Right Handed Quilters

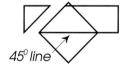 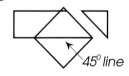

45⁰ line   *45⁰ line*

E - Cut 1 - 6 ¹/₄" square, light. (3 ³/₄")
Cut in half diagonally, twice.

F - Cut 4 - 4" squares, light. (2 ¹/₄")

Arrows show pressing direction.

1. Sew **A** to **A1**. Press. Cut off the dog ears. Make four sets.

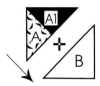

2. Sew the **A/A1** set to **B**. Cut off the dog ears. Press. Make four sets.

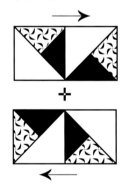

3. Following the diagram, butt, pin, sew and press into pairs. Then sew the pairs together. It doesn't matter which way you press the center seam.

4. Sew **C** to **D**. Stop sewing ¹/₄″ from the bottom edge and back tack. You will press this seam when you are butting to the middle section in # 5 and #7. Make four sets.

Stop sewing ¹/₄″ and back tack

5. Press the **C/D** seam opposite of the pinwheel seam. Butt, pin and sew one **C/D** set to each end of the pinwheel unit. Press to the **C/D** set.

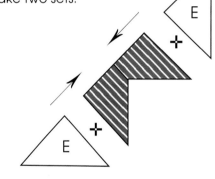

6. Sew one E to each end of the **C/D** set. Press to the **C/D** set. Cut off the dog ears. Make two sets.

7. Press the **C/D** seam opposite of the pinwheel seam. Butt, pin and sew the side sections to the pinwheel unit. Press to the side sections. Cut off the dog ears.

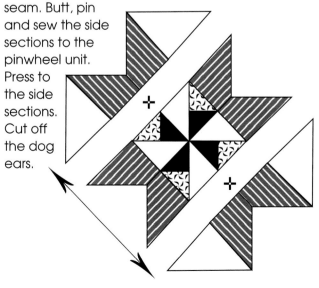

8. Set in the **F** squares according to the directions on page 9. Press to the **F** squares.

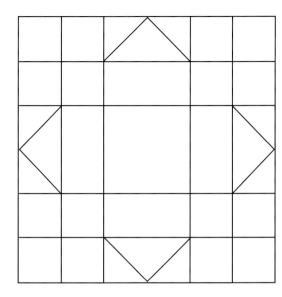

Block Size:
12" (or 6") finished

Seam Allowance:
¼"

**Full Size
Quilt Guide:
Page 63**

Photo on Page 37

Identifying the Shapes

A, B, F - Square
C - Half Square Triangle
D - Quarter Square Triangle
E - Rectangle

Rotary Cutting Directions

Numbers in parentheses are for the 6" block.

A - Cut 1 - 2 ½" x 22" strip, light. (1 ½" x 13")

B - Cut 1 - 2 ½" x 22" strip, dark. (1 ½" x 13")

C - Cut 4 - 2 ⅞" squares, medium light. (1 ⅞")
Cut in half diagonally, once.

D - Cut 1 - 5 ¼" square, dark. (3 ¼")
Cut in half diagonally, twice.

E - Cut 4 - 2 ½" x 4 ½" rectangles, dark.
(1 ½" x 2 ½")

F - Cut 1 - 4 ½" square, medium light. (2 ½")

Sewing Directions

Arrows show pressing direction.

1. Sew strip **A** to strip **B**. Press. Cut the sewn strips into eight 2 ½" sections. (1 ½")

2. Butt, pin and sew the **A/B** sections together. Press. Make two units of each.

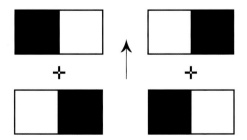

3. Sew one **C** to **D**. Press. Sew **C** to the other side of **D**. Press. Cut off the dog ears. Make four sets.

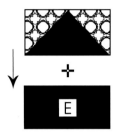

4. Sew the **C/D** set to **E**. Press. Make four units.

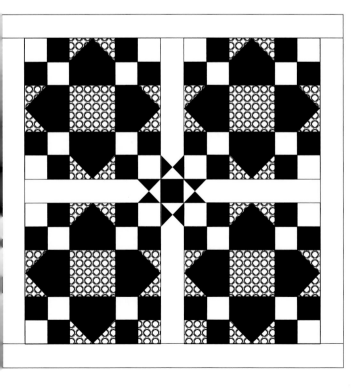

5. Butt, pin and sew into rows. Press according to the diagram. Butt, pin and sew the rows together. Press according to the side arrows.

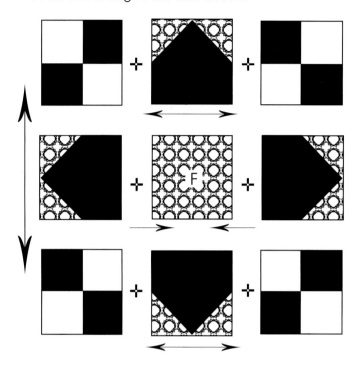

A stunning quilt could easily be made by just using three colors and jazzing up the lattice strips.

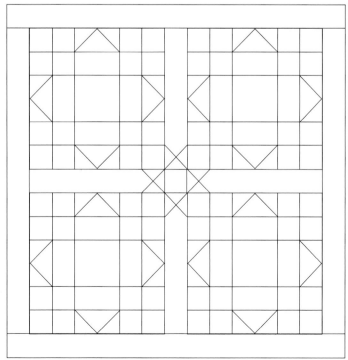

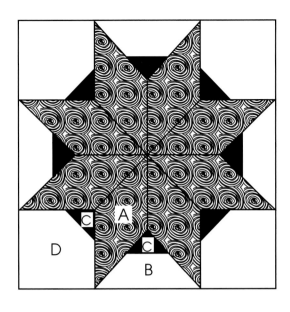

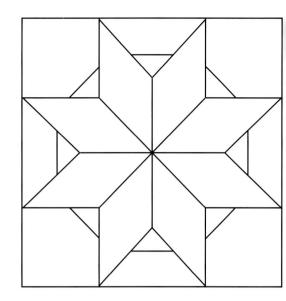

Block Size:
12" (or 6") finished

Seam Allowance:
¼"

Full Size
Quilt Guide:
Page 63

Photo on Page 34

Identifying the Shapes

A - 45° Diamond
B - Full Trapezoid
C - Half Square Triangle
D - Clipped Square

Rotary Cutting Directions

Numbers in parentheses are for the 6" block.

A - Cut 1 - 3" x 37" strip, medium dark.
(1 ³/4" x 24") Cut into eight 3" - 45° diamonds.
(1 ³/4") See the diagram.

Left Handed Quilters   Right Handed Quilters

B - Cut 4 - 1 3/4" x 6 1/4" rectangles, light.
(1 1/8" x 3 3/4") To recut into a full trapezoid, use
a 6" square Omnigrid® ruler. Place the ruler so
the 45° line is in the corner of the rectangle.
Also keep the 45° line on the bottom of the

rectangle. Cut off the excess fabric. Slide the
ruler to the other corner of the rectangle and
cut off the excess fabric.

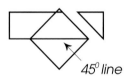   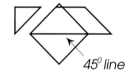

45⁰ line   *45⁰ line*

C - Cut 4 - 2 ⁵/8" squares, dark. (1 ³/4")
Cut in half diagonally, once.

D - Cut 4 - 4" squares, light. (2 1/4") To cut a clipped
square, place the ruler so the 1 1/2" marking runs
diagonally through the square. (⁷/8")
Cut off the excess fabric.

Left Handed Quilters   Right Handed Quilters

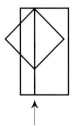   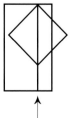

1 ¹/2" marking   *1 ¹/2" marking*
(⁷/8")   *(⁷/8")*

Sewing Directions

Arrows show pressing direction.

1. Sew one **A** to another **A**. Stop sewing $1/4''$ from the bottom edge and back tack. Press according to the diagram. Cut off the dog ears. Make four sets.

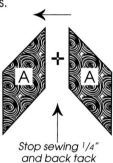

Stop sewing $1/4''$ and back tack

2. Butt, pin and sew two sets together. Stop sewing $1/4''$ from the bottom edge and back tack. Press according to the diagram. Make two sets.

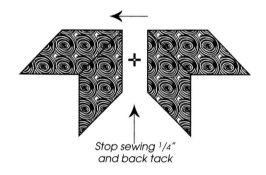

Stop sewing $1/4''$ and back tack

3. Butt and pin the two halves together. Start sewing in from the left edge $1/4''$. Sew only two stitches, back tack and then continue sewing until you are $1/4''$ from the end. Back tack. It doesn't matter which way you press the center seam.

Start sewing in $1/4''$ and back tack

Stop sewing $1/4''$ and back tack

4. Sew **C** to **B**. Press. Cut off the dog ears. Make four units.

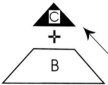

5. Set in the **B/C** triangles according to the directions on page 9. Press to the **B/C** triangle.

6. Sew **C** to **D**. Press. Cut off the dog ears. Make four units.

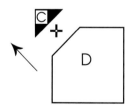

7. Set in the **C/D** squares according to the directions on page 9. Press to **C/D**.

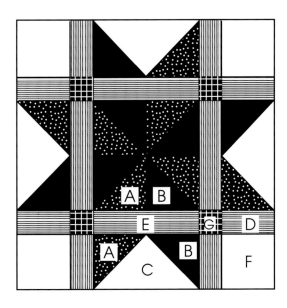

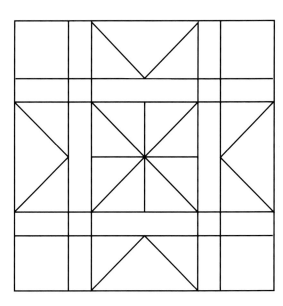

Block Size:
12" (or 6") finished

Seam Allowance:
¼"

Full Size
Quilt Guide:
Page 63

Photo on Page 35

Identifying the Shapes

A, B - Half Square Triangle
C - Quarter Square Triangle
D, E - Rectangle
F, G - Square

Rotary Cutting Directions

Numbers in parentheses are for the 6" block.

A - Cut 4 - 3 ³/₈" squares, medium dark. (2 ¹/₈")
Cut in half diagonally, once.

B - Cut 4 - 3 ³/₈" squares, dark. (2 ¹/₈") Cut in half
diagonally, once.

C - Cut 1 - 6 ¹/₄" square, light. (3 ³/₄") Cut in half
diagonally, twice.

D - Cut 8 - 1 ¹/₂" x 3" rectangles, medium light.
(1" x 1 ³/₄")

E - Cut 4 - 1 ¹/₂" x 5 ¹/₂" rectangles, medium light.
(1" x 3")

F - Cut 4 - 3" squares, light. (1 ³/₄")

G - Cut 4 - 1 ¹/₂" squares, contrasting dark. (1")

Sewing Directions

Arrows show pressing direction.

1. Sew one **A** to **C**. Press. Sew **B** to the other side of **C**.
   Press. Cut off the dog ears. Make four sets.

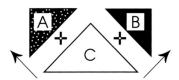

2. Sew **A** to **B**. Cut off the dog ears. Press.
   Make four sets.

3. Following the diagram, butt, pin, sew and press into pairs. Then sew the pairs together. It doesn't matter which way you press the center seam.

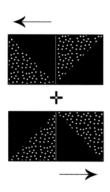

4. Butt, pin and sew into rows. Press according to the diagram. Butt, pin and sew the rows together. Press **Row 1** and **3** towards **Row 2**.

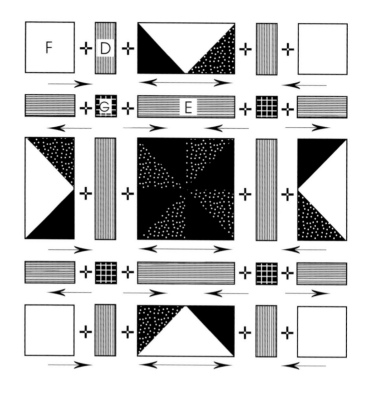

A secondary design is formed when four Star Lane blocks are sewn together.

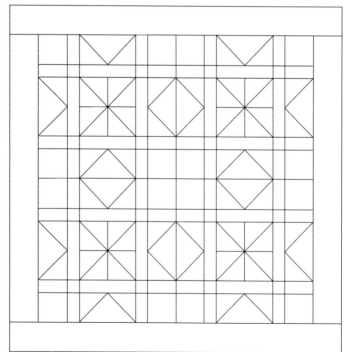

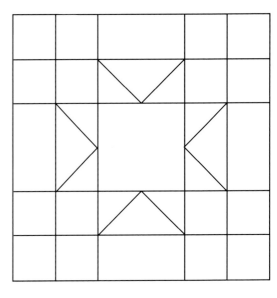

Block Size:
12" (or 6") finished

Seam Allowance:
¼"

**Full Size
Quilt Guide:**
Page 64

Photo on Page 36

Identifying the Shapes

A, B, C, G - Square

D - Half Square Triangle

E - Quarter Square Triangle

F - Rectangle

Rotary Cutting Directions

Numbers in parentheses are for the 6" block.

A - Cut 1 - 2 ¹/₂" x 12" strip, light. (1 ¹/₂" x 8")

B - Cut 2 - 2 1/2" x 12" strip, medium light.
     (1 ¹/₂" x 8")

C - Cut 1 - 2 1/2" x 12" strip, dark. (1 ¹/₂" x 8")

D - Cut 4 - 2 ⁷/₈" squares, light. (1 ⁷/₈")
     Cut in half diagonally, once.

E - Cut 1 - 5 ¹/₄" square, dark. (3 ¹/₄")
     Cut in half diagonally, twice.

F - Cut 4 - 2 ¹/₂" x 4 ¹/₂" rectangles, dark.
     (1 ¹/₂" x 2 ¹/₂")

G - Cut 1 - 4 ¹/₂" square, light. (2 ¹/₂")

Sewing Directions

Arrows show pressing direction.

1. Sew strip **A** to strip **B**. Press. Sew strip **B** to strip **C**. Press. Cut each set of sewn strips into four 2 ¹/₂" sections. (1 ¹/₂")

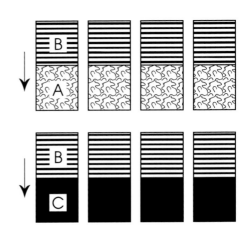

2. Butt, pin and sew an **A/B** section to a **B/C** section. Press. Make two units of each.

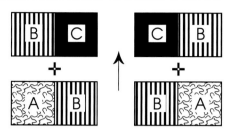

3. Sew one **D** to **E**. Press. Sew **D** to the other side of **E**. Press. Cut off the dog ears. Make four sets.

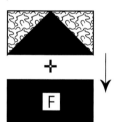

4. Sew **F** to the **D/E** section. Press. Make four units.

5. Butt, pin and sew into rows. Press according to the diagram. Butt, pin and sew the rows together. Press according to the side arrows.

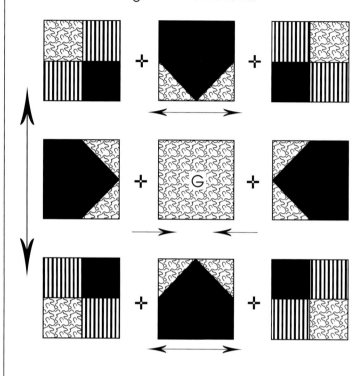

Creating a scrappy look with the Star Surrounded block would be very easy.
Simply make all the stars a different color.

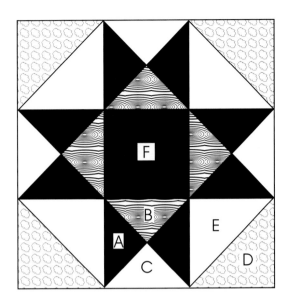

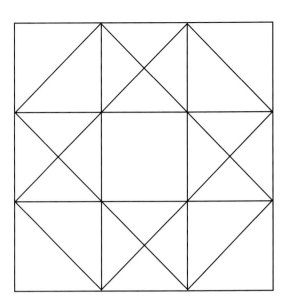

Block Size:
12" (or 6") finished

Seam Allowance:
¼"

Full Size
Quilt Guide:
Page 64

Photo on Page 37

Identifying the Shapes

A, B, C - Quarter Square Triangle
D, E - Half Square Triangle
F - Square

Rotary Cutting Directions

Numbers in parentheses are for the 6" block.

A - Cut 2 - 5 ¼" squares, dark. (3 ¼") Cut in half diagonally, twice.

B - Cut 1 - 5 ¼" square, medium dark. (3 ¼") Cut in half diagonally, twice.

C - Cut 1 - 5 ¼" square, light. (3 ¼") Cut in half diagonally, twice.

D - Cut 2 - 4 ⅞" squares, medium light. (2 ⅞") Cut in half diagonally, once.

E - Cut 2 - 4 ⅞" squares, light. (2 ⅞") Cut in half diagonally, once.

F - Cut 1 - 4 ½" square, dark. (2 ½")

Sewing Directions

Arrows show pressing direction.

1. Sew **A** to **B**. Press. Sew **A** to **C**. Press. Cut off the dog ears. Make four sets of each.

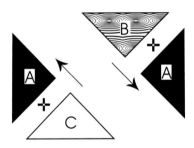

2. Sew one **A/B** set to one **A/C** set. Press. Cut off the dog ears. Make four units.

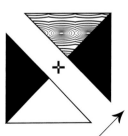

3. Sew **D** to **E**. Press. Cut off the dog ears. Make four sets.

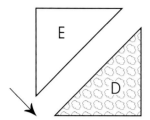

4. Butt, pin and sew into rows. Press according to the diagram. Butt, pin and sew the rows together. Press according to the side arrows.

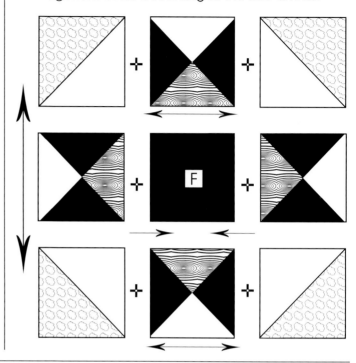

A wonderful original way of setting the Swamp Patch blocks together.

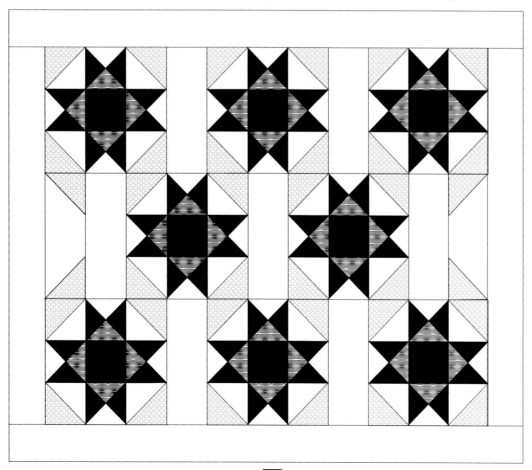

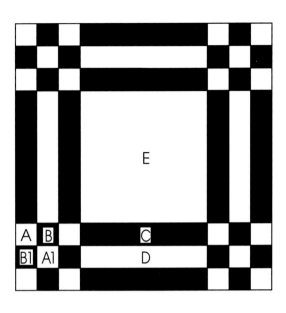

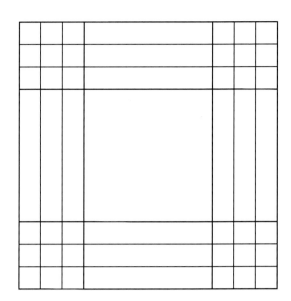

Block Size:
12" (or 6") finished

Seam Allowance:
¼"

Full Size
Quilt Guide:
Page 64

Photo on Page 36

Identifying the Shapes

A, A1 B, B1, E - Square
C, D - Rectangle

Rotary Cutting Directions

Numbers in parentheses are for the 6" block.

A - Cut 2 - 1 ½" x 14" strips, light. (1" x 10")

A1 - Cut 1 - 1 ½" X 7" strip, light. (1" x 5")

B - Cut 1 - 1 ½" x 14" strip, dark. (1" x 10")

B1 - Cut 2 - 1 ½" x 7" strips, dark. (1" x 5")

C - Cut 2 - 1 ½" x 28" strips, dark. (1" x 15")

D - Cut 1 - 1 ½" x 28" strip, light. (1" x 15")

E - Cut 1 - 6 ½" square, light. (3 ½")

Note: Another option for the 12" block is to use one of the 6 ½" unfinished blocks from this book.

Sewing Directions

Arrows show pressing direction.

1. Following the diagrams, sew the proper strips together. Press. Cut Set 1 into eight 1 ½" (1") sections. Cut Set 2 into four 1 ½" (1") sections.

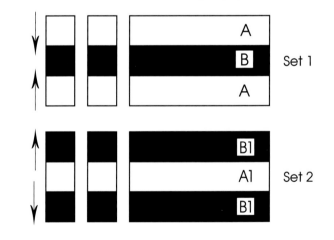

2. Butt, pin and sew two cut sections from Set 1 to one cut section from Set 2. Press. Make four units.

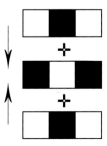

3. Sew one **C** strip to **D**. Press. Sew another **C** strip to **D**. Press. Cut the sewn strips into four 6 ½" (3 ½") sections.

4. Butt, pin and sew into rows. Press according to the diagram. Butt, pin and sew the rows together. Press according to the side arrows.

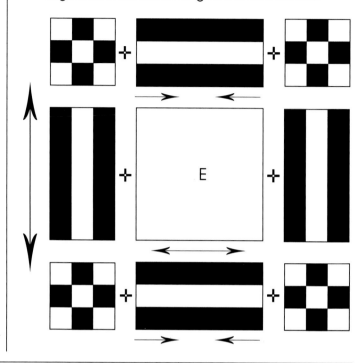

An exciting quilt is created by using the 12" Tic Tac Toe block with 6" Star of Dreams for the centers.

Sewing Directions

Row 1: Follow the diagram for sewing the lattice strips to the blocks. Press to the lattice strips. Make 6 rows.

Row 2: Follow the diagram for sewing the lattice strips to the cornerstones. Press to the lattice strips. Make 5 rows. Butt, pin and sew the rows together. Press to the lattice strips. Add side borders. Press. Add top and bottom border. Press. The quilt will measure 83" x 98" unquilted.

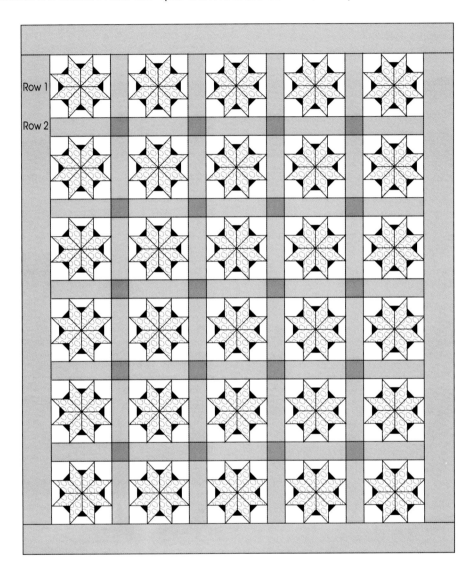

BORDERS, LATTICE STRIPS, CORNERSTONES
Piecing Diagram Shown Above

FABRIC	NUMBER OF STRIPS	TOTAL PIECES NEEDED
Medium Dark - 4 1/2 yds.		
Side Borders	2 - 6" x 92" strips	Extra length has been added Cut to the desired length later
Top and Bottom Border	2 - 6" x 89" strips	Extra length has been added Cut to the desired length later
Lattice Strips	17 - 3 1/2" x 40" strips	49 - 3 1/2" x 12 1/2" strips
Dark - 3/8 yd.		
Cornerstones	2 - 3 1/2" strips	20 - 3 1/2" squares
Binding	Use the remaining fabric	

After making one sample block of the desired 12" pattern, you are now ready to make a full size quilt. The yardage below is given for a quilt consisting of 30 blocks made from the same pattern (5 across, 6 down) set with 3" finished lattice strips, 3" finished cornerstones and 5 1/2" finished borders. The quilt will measure 83" x 98" unquilted. A graphic and how to assemble the quilt is shown on page 58. The yardage given for each color is based upon 40" wide fabric. <u>Because of shrinkage and resquaring of the fabric, I have added extra yardage to each color.</u>

How To Use the Full Size Quilt Guide: The yardage is given for each color in Column 1. Read across to Column 2 for the number of required strips . Column 3 tells you the total number of pieces needed to make 30 blocks. <u>Follow the pattern for recutting the strips into the desired shapes.</u> For example: Friendship Star - A - Cut 8 - 4 $^7/_8$" x 40" strips. Recut the strips into 60 - 4 $^7/_8$" squares. Refer back to the pattern on page 12 and you will see you need to cut the 4 $^7/_8$" squares in half diagonally.

FABRIC	NUMBER OF STRIPS	TOTAL PIECES NEEDED

FRIENDSHIP STAR
Pattern on Page 12   Colored Photo on Page 36

FABRIC	NUMBER OF STRIPS	TOTAL PIECES NEEDED
Medium Dark - 1 $^1/_4$ yds..............................	**A** - 8 - 4 $^7/_8$" x 40" strips	60 - 4 $^7/_8$" Squares
Light - 3 $^1/_4$ yds.	**B** - 8 - 4 $^7/_8$" x 40" strips	60 - 4 $^7/_8$" Squares
....	**C** - 15 - 4 $^1/_2$" x 40" strips	120 - 4 $^1/_2$" Squares
Dark - $^3/_4$ yds.	**D** - 4 - 4 $^1/_2$" x 40" strips	30 - 4 $^1/_2$" Squares

MONKEY WRENCH
Pattern on Page 13   Colored Photo on Page 35

FABRIC	NUMBER OF STRIPS	TOTAL PIECES NEEDED
Light - 3 yds..	**A** - 6 - 3 $^7/_8$" x 40" strips	60 - 3 $^7/_8$" Squares
....	**C** - 20 - 2" x 40" strips......................	120 - 2" X 6 $^1/_2$" Rectangles
....	**E** - 5 - 6 $^1/_2$" x 40" strips	30 - 6 $^1/_2$" Squares
Dark - 2 yds..	**B** - 6 - 3 $^7/_8$" x 40" strips	60 - 3 $^7/_8$" Squares
....	**D** - 20 - 2" x 40" strips......................	120 - 2" X 6 $^1/_2$" Rectangles

JACOB'S LADDER
Pattern on Page 14   Colored Photo on Page 35

FABRIC	NUMBER OF STRIPS	TOTAL PIECES NEEDED
Medium Dark - $^3/_4$ yd.	**A** - 8 - 2 $^1/_2$" x 40" strips	120 - 2 $^1/_2$" Squares
Medium Light - 1 $^5/_8$ yds................................	**B** - 8 - 2 $^1/_2$" x 40" strips	120 - 2 $^1/_2$" Squares
....	**B1**- 12 - 2 $^1/_2$" x 40" strips	180 - 2 $^1/_2$" Squares
Light - 2 $^1/_4$ yds.	**C** - 12 - 2 $^1/_2$" x 40" strips	180 - 2 $^1/_2$" Squares
....	**D** - 8 - 4 $^7/_8$" x 40" strips	60 - 4 $^7/_8$" Squares
Dark - 1 $^3/_8$ yds.	**E** - 8 - 4 $^7/_8$" x 40" strips	60 - 4 $^7/_8$" Squares

SQUARES AND TRIANGLES
Pattern on Page 16   Colored Photo on Page 34

Medium Light - 1 1/2 yds. ....**A** - 12 - 3 7/8" x 40" strips ....120 - 3 7/8" Squares

Medium Dark - 7/8 yd. ....**B** - 6 - 3 7/8" x 40" strips .... 60 - 3 7/8" Squares

Contrasting
Medium Dark - 7/8 yd. ....**C** - 6 - 3 7/8" x 40" strips .... 60 - 3 7/8" Squares

Light - 7/8 yd. ....**D** - 6 - 3 7/8"x 40" strips .... 60 - 3 7/8" Squares

Dark - 1 7/8 yds. ....**E** - 4 - 4 3/4" x 40" strips .... 30 - 4 3/4" Squares
....**F** - 11 - 3 1/2" x 40" strips ....120 - 3 1/2" Squares

AMHERST STAR
Pattern on Page 18   Colored Photo on Page 34

Dark - 3/4 yd. ....**A** - 8 - 2 3/8" x 40" strips ....120 - 2 3/8" Squares

Medium Dark - 2 1/4 yds. ....**B** - 20 - 2 1/2" x 40" strips ....240 - 2 1/2" x 3 1/8" Rectangles
.....................................**F** - 6 - 3 3/8" x 40" strips .... 60 - 3 3/8" Squares

Light - 2 1/2 yds. ....**C** - 5 - 6 1/4" x 40" strips .... 30 - 6 1/4" Squares
.....................................**G** - 12 - 4" x 40" strips.....................120 - 4" Squares

Medium Light - 1 yd. ....**D** - 3 - 3 1/4" x 40" strips .... 30 - 3 1/4" Squares
.....................................**E** - 4 - 4 1/16" x 40" strips .... 30 - 4 1/16" Squares

BURSTING STAR
Pattern on Page 20   Colored Photo on Page 35

Light - 1 3/8 yds. ....**A** - 14 - 2 7/8" x 40" strips ....180 - 2 7/8" Squares

Dark - 2 1/4 yds. ....**B** - 19 - 2 7/8" x 40" strips ....240 - 2 7/8" Squares
.....................................**F** - 4 - 4 1/2" x 40" strips .... 30 - 4 1/2" Squares

Medium Dark - 1 yd. ....**C** - 10 - 2 7/8" x 40" strips ....120 - 2 7/8" Square

Medium Light - 2 1/2 yds. ....**D** - 5 - 2 7/8" x 40" strips .... 60 - 2 7/8" Squares
.....................................**E** - 15 - 4 1/2" x 40" strips ....120 - 4 1/2" x 4 5/8" Rectangles

FABRIC	NUMBER OF STRIPS	TOTAL PIECES NEEDED

CAMPBELL HOUSE
Pattern on Page 22   Colored Photo on Page 36

Medium Dark - 2 1/2 yds.	**A** - 15 - 1 1/2" x 40" strips	120 - 1 1/2" x 4 1/2" Rectangles
	C - 4 - 1 3/4" x 40" strips	60 - 1 3/4" x 2 1/2" Rectangles
	E - 10 - 1 1/2" x 40" strips	30 - 1 1/2" x 10 1/2" Rectangles
	G - 3 - 1 1/2" x 40" strips	60 - 1 1/2" Squares
	H - 22 - 1 1/2" x 40" strips	240 - 1 1/2" x 3 1/2" Rectangles
Medium Light - 7/8 yd.	**B** - 5 - 2 1/2" x 40" strips	60 - 2 1/2" x 3 1/4" Rectangles
	F - 5 - 1 1/2" x 40" strips	120 - 1 1/2" Squares
Dark - 1/2 yd.	**D** - 4 - 2 1/2" x 40" strips	30 - 2 1/2" x 4 1/2" Rectangles
Light - 1 3/4 yds.	**I** - 15 - 1 1/2" x 40" strips	60 - 1 1/2" x 8 1/2" Rectangles
	J - 3 - 3 3/8" x 40" strips	30 - 3 3/8" Squares
	L - 5 - 2" x 40" strips	60 - 2" x 3" Rectangles
	N - 4 - 2" x 40" strips	30 - 2" x 4 1/2" Rectangles
Constrasting Dark - 1 1/8 yds.	**K** - 10 - 3" x 40" strips	30 - 3" x 13 1/4" Rectangles
Contrasting Medium Dark - 3/8 yd.	**M** - 3 - 2" x 40" strips	60 - 2" Squares

CHECKERED STAR
Pattern on Page 24   Colored Photo on Page 35

Dark - 2 yds.	**A** - 11 - 1 3/4" x 40" strips	240 - 1 3/4" Squares
	C1 - 10 - 1 3/4" x 40" strips	120 - 1 3/4" x 3 1/8" Rectangles
	D - 14 - 1 3/4" x 40" strips	120 - 1 3/4" x 4 3/8" Rectangles
Medium Dark - 2 yds.	**B** - 11 - 1 3/4" x 40" strips	240 - 1 3/4" Squares
	C - 10 - 1 3/4" x 40" strips	120 - 1 3/4" x 3 1/8" Rectangles
	D1 - 14 - 1 3/4" x 40" strips	120 - 1 3/4" x 4 3/8" Rectangles
Light - 2 1/2 yds.	**E** - 5 - 6 1/4" x 40" strips	30 - 6 1/4" Squares
	F - 12 - 4" x 40" strips	120 - 4" Squares

DOUBLE POINTED STAR
Pattern on Page 26   Colored Photo on Page 34

Dark - 1 yd.	**A** - 10 - 2 7/8" x 40" strips	120 - 2 7/8" Squares
Medium Light - 3 yds.	**B** - 5 - 5 1/4" x 40" strips	30 - 5 1/4" Squares
	F - 15 - 4 1/2" x 40" strips	120 - 4 1/2" Squares
Medium Dark - 1 5/8 yds.	**C** - 10 - 2 7/8" x 40" x strips	120 - 2 7/8" Squares
	G - 4 - 4 1/2" x 40" strips	30 - 4 1/2" Squares
Light - 1 3/8 yds	**D** - 5 - 5 1/4" x 40" strips	30 - 5 1/4" Squares
	E - 5 - 2 7/8" x 40" strips	60 - 2 7/8" Squares

FABRIC	NUMBER OF STRIPS	TOTAL PIECES NEEDED

FERRIS WHEEL
Pattern on Page 28   Colored Photo on Page 34

Dark - 2 1/8 yds. ....**A** - 30 - 2 1/4" x 40" strips ....240 - 2 1/4" x 4 7/8" Rectangles

Light - 3 yds..**A1**- 30 - 2 1/4" x 40" strips ....240 - 2 1/4" x 4 7/8" Rectangles

....**C** - 7 - 4 3/8" x 40" strips .... 60 - 4 3/8" Squares

Medium Dark - 1 1/4 yds.....................................**B** - 11 - 3 3/8" x 40" strips ....120 - 3 3/8" Squares

INDIAN HEAD
Pattern on Page 30   Colored Photo on Page 35

Light - 1 1/8 yds. ....**A** - 5 - 6 1/2" x 40" strips .... 30 - 6 1/2" Squares

Dark - 1 5/8 yds. ....**B** - 9 - 5 1/8" x 40" strips................. 60 - 5 1/8" Squares

Medium Dark - 1 3/4 yds. ....**C** - 9 - 5 1/2" x 40" strips .... 60 - 5 1/2" Squares

Medium Light - 1 5/8 yds. ....**D** - 15 - 3" x 40" strips.....................120 - 3" x 4 7/8" Rectangles

LOVE APPLE STAR
Pattern on Page 32   Colored Photo on Page 36

Dark - 3 1/2 yds. ....**A** - 10 - 2 1/2" x 40" strips ....120 - 45° Parallelograms

....**A1**- 10 - 2 1/2" x 40" strips ....120 - 45° Parallelograms

....**D** - 8 - 4 7/8" x 40" strips .... 60 - 4 7/8" Squares

....**F** - 4 - 4 1/2" x 40" strips .... 30 - 4 1/2" Squares

Medium Dark - 1 yd..**B** - 10 - 2 7/8" x 40" strips ....120 - 2 7/8" Squares

Light - 2 1/8 yds. ....**C** - 5 - 5 1/4" x 40" strips .... 30 - 5 1/4" Squares

....**E** - 8 - 4 7/8" x 40" strips .... 60 - 4 7/8" Squares

PEEK A BOO STAR
Pattern on Page 42   Colored Photo on Page 36

Light - 2 7/8 yds. ....**A** - 20 - 1 3/4" x 40" strips ....120 - 1 3/4" x 6 1/4" Rectangles

....**D** - 3 - 3 1/4" x 40" strips .... 30 - 3 1/4" Squares

....**E** - 12 - 4" x 40" strips.....................120 - 4" Squares

Dark - 7/8 yd...**B** - 8 - 2 5/8" x 40" strips ....120 - 2 5/8" Squares

Medium Dark - 2 7/8 yds. ....**C** - 14 - 4 3/8" x 40" strips ....120 - 4 3/8" Square

....**F** - 5 - 5 1/2" x 40" strips .... 30 - 5 1/2" Squares

FABRIC	NUMBER OF STRIPS	TOTAL PIECES NEEDED

PINWHEEL STAR
Pattern on Page 44   Colored Photo on Page 34

Contrasting
Medium Dark - 1/2 yd. ....**A** - 3 - 3 3/4" x 40" strips .... 30 - 3 3/4" Squares

Dark - 1/2 yd. ....**A1**- 3 - 3 3/4" x 40" strips .... 30 - 3 3/4" Squares

Light - 3 1/8 yds. ....**B** - 6 - 3 3/8" x 40" strips .... 60 - 3 3/8" Squares
....**E** - 5 - 6 1/4" x 40" strips .... 30 - 6 1/4" Squares
....**F** - 12 - 4" x 40" strips.....................120 - 4" Squares

Medium Dark - 2 5/8 yds. ....**C** - 14 - 3" x 40" strips.....................120 - 3" x 4 3/8" Rectangles
....**D** - 14 - 3" x 40" strips.....................120 - 3" x 4 3/8" Rectangles

SQUARE WITHIN
Pattern on Page 46   Colored Photo on Page 37

Light - 1 1/4 yds. ....**A** - 15 - 2 1/2" x 40" strips ....240 - 2 1/2" Squares

Dark - 3 1/8 yds. ....**B** - 15 - 2 1/2" x 40" strips ....240 - 2 1/2" Squares
....**D** - 5 - 5 1/4" x 40" strips .... 30 - 5 1/4" Squares
....**E** - 15 - 2 1/2" x 40" strips ....120 - 2 1/2" x 4 1/2" Rectangles

Medium Light - 1 1/2 yds. ....**C** - 10 - 2 7/8" x 40" strips ....120 - 2 7/8" Squares
....**F** - 4 - 4 1/2" x 40" strips .... 30 - 4 1/2" Squares

STAR OF DREAMS
Pattern on Page 48   Colored Photo on Page 34

Medium Dark - 2 1/2 yds. ....**A** - 27 - 3" x 40" strips.....................240 - 3" - 45° Diamonds

Light - 2 5/8 yds. ....**B** - 20 - 1 3/4" x 40" strips ....120 - 1 3/4" x 6 1/4" Rectangles
....**D** - 12 - 4" x 40" strips.....................120 - 4" Squares

Dark - 3/4 yd. ....**C** - 8 - 2 5/8" x 40" strips ....120 - 2 5/8" Squares

STAR LANE
Pattern on Page 50   Colored Photo on Page 35

Medium Dark - 1 1/4 yds. ....**A** - 11 - 3 3/8"x 40" strips ....120 - 3 3/8" Squares

Dark - 1 1/4 yds. ....**B** - 11 - 3 3/8" x 40" strips ....120 - 3 3/8" Squares

Light - 2 yds. ....**C** - 5 - 6 1/4" x 40" strips .... 30 - 6 1/4" Squares
....**F** - 10 - 3" x 40" strips.....................120 - 3" Squares

Medium Light - 1 3/4 yds. ....**D** - 19 - 1 1/2" x 40" strips ....240 - 1 1/2" x 3" Rectangles
....**E** - 18 - 1 1/2" x 40" strips ....120 - 1 1/2" x 5 1/2" Rectangles

Contrasting Dark - 3/8 yd. ....**G** - 5 - 1 1/2" x 40" strips ....120 - 1 1/2" Squares

STAR SURROUNDED
Pattern on Page 52   Colored Photo on Page 36

Light - 2 1/4 yds. ....**A** - 8 - 2 1/2" x 40" strips ....120 - 2 1/2" Squares
....**D** - 10 - 2 7/8" x 40" strips ....120 - 2 7/8" Squares
....**G** - 4 - 4 1/2" x 40" strips .... 30 - 4 1/2" Squares

Medium Light - 1 1/4 yds. ....**B** - 15 - 2 1/2" x 40" strips ....240 - 2 1/2" Squares

Dark - 2 5/8 yds. ....**C** - 8 - 2 1/2" x 40" strips ....120 - 2 1/2" Squares
....**E** - 5 - 5 1/4" x 40" strips .... 30 - 5 1/4" Squares
....**F** - 15 - 2 1/2" x 40" strips ....120 - 2 1/2" x 4 1/2" Rectangles

SWAMP PATCH
Pattern on Page 54   Colored Photo on Page 37

Dark - 2 1/8 yds. ....**A** - 9 - 5 1/4" x 40" strips ....60 - 5 1/4" Squares
....**F** - 4 - 4 1/2" x 40" strips ....30 - 4 1/2" Squares

Medium Dark - 1 yd. ....**B** - 5 - 5 1/4" x 40" strips ....30 - 5 1/4" Squares

Light - 2 1/8 yds. ....**C** - 5 - 5 1/4" x 40" strips ....30 - 5 1/4" Squares
....**E** - 8 - 4 7/8" x 40" strips ....60 - 4 7/8" Squares

Medium Light - 1 3/8 yds. ....**D** - 8 - 4 7/8" x 40" strips ....60 - 4 7/8" Squares

TIC TAC TOE
Pattern on Page 56   Colored Photo on Page 36

Light - 3 1/8 yds. ....**A** - 19 - 1 1/2" x 40" strips ....480 - 1 1/2" Squares
....**A1** - 5 - 1 1/2" x 40" strips ....120 - 1 1/2" Squares
....**D** - 20 - 1 1/2" x 40" strips ....120 - 1 1/2" x 6 1/2" Rectangles
....**E** - 5 - 6 1/2" x 40" strips .... 30 - 6 1/2" Squares

Dark - 2 7/8 yds. ....**B** - 10 - 1 1/2" x 40" strips ....240 - 1 1/2" Squares
....**B1** - 10 - 1 1/2" x 40" strips ....240 - 1 1/2" Squares
....**C** - 40 - 1 1/2" x 40" strips ....240 - 1 1/2" x 6 1/2" Rectangles

About The Author

Nancy Johnson-Srebro is an internationally known quilt teacher, lecturer, author and show judge. She is a prolific author, having written *Miniature to Masterpiece*, *Timeless Treasures*, *Featherweight 221*, *Add On Seam Allowance Chart*, *Measure The Possibilities with Omnigrid*, and the *NO-FAIL™ Fabric Yardage Chart*. Nancy's books and her NO-FAIL™ techniques have become standard texts for rotary cutting and precision piecing. She lectures and teaches extensively, sharing her love of quiltmaking with other quilters.

Photo: Scott Mowry